THE DECISIVE BATTLE OF NASHVILLE

THE DECISIVE
BATTLE OF
NASHVILLE

STANLEY F. HORN

LOUISIANA STATE UNIVERSITY PRESS

Baton Rouge and London

LIBRARY OF CONGRESS CATALOG CARD NUMBER:
56-12173
ISBN: 0-8071-1709-9 (paper)

Louisiana Paperback Edition, 1991
00 99 98 97 96 95 94 93 92 91   5 4 3 2 1

Preface

THE battle of Nashville, according to one distinguished military authority, "has been generally accepted as a perfect exemplification of the art of war." Another authority has said: "No battle of the war was better planned, and none was so nearly carried out to the letter of the plan as the battle of Nashville. It has been said that this plan of Thomas is the only one of the entire war that is now studied as a model in European military schools." In pointing out these distinguishing features of the battle fought at Nashville in December of 1864, the high water mark of the Southern Confederacy's last aggressive action, these authorities might also have pointed out that it was the decisive battle of the Civil War, for such it was. Indeed, one historian has referred to it as "a victory unprecedented in its decisiveness."[1]

Just what, it may be asked, is a decisive battle? Sir Edward Creasy in his *Fifteen Decisive Battles of the World* gives us a definition which may be accepted as authoritative. A decisive battle, Creasy says, is a battle "of which a contrary event would have essentially varied the drama of the world in all its subsequent scenes."[2]

Creasy's definition is exacting in its terms. After all,

[1] John M. Schofield, *Forty-six Years in the Army* (New York, 1897), 248; Francis T. Miller (ed.), *The Photographic History of the Civil War*, 10 vols. (New York, 1912), III, 264; Thomas B. Van Horne, *The Life of Major General George H. Thomas* (New York, 1882), 349 (hereinafter referred to as *Life of Thomas*).

[2] Sir Edward S. Creasy, *The Fifteen Decisive Battles of the World* (New York, 1931).

few battles have been of such a nature as to vary "the drama of the world" by their outcome. Considering the present position of world power occupied by the United States, however, it seems safe to say that any battle which definitely affected the history of this country did, correspondingly, affect the history of the world. Obviously, therefore, any battle which exerted a really decisive influence on the outcome of the Civil War must be considered a decisive battle in the widest application of that term.

What, then, was the decisive engagement of the great war that shook our country for the four years from 1861 to 1865? The question, it should be observed, is not which battle had the most men engaged, or which involved the most prominent commanders, or which had the greatest casualties or received the greatest publicity. The question is: Which battle, by a contrary event, would have influenced the final result of the war and thereby "varied the drama of the world"?

It is an impressive fact that, aside from the battle of Nashville, all the engagements of the Civil War were strangely indecisive. The first full-scale clash at Bull Run resulted in the complete victory of the Confederate army and the total defeat and rout of the Federal forces—but it was in no sense a decisive battle, because nothing came of it. The Confederates rested complacently on their laurels, giving the Federals ample time to patch together the pieces of their broken army and prepare for another campaign. Then, the following summer, Lee administered a stinging, but again indecisive, defeat to McClellan in the battles around Richmond. Came another long wait, and then another brilliant victory for the Confederates at Second Manassas—but the war went right ahead.

Meanwhile, in the West, there had been the bloody

battle of Shiloh—but, for all its shocking toll of dead
and wounded, it decided nothing. Other battles, accompanied by great bloodshed and loss of life, followed
as the months and years went by: Perryville, Murfreesboro, Chickamauga, Missionary Ridge, and Atlanta in
the West; Sharpsburg, Fredericksburg, Chancellorsville,
Gettysburg, the Wilderness, and Cold Harbor in the
East. All these famous major engagements were bitterly
contested, with staggering losses on both sides. But they
were none of them decisive. Following each there was
a lull for reinforcement, refreshment, and preparation,
and then the two adversaries were at each other's throats
again. And so the war dragged on—until the battle of
Nashville, the climactic engagement. After Nashville
there were no more battles of material import. Within
four months the war was over.

The supreme significance and importance of the
battle of Nashville may be better appreciated when it is
borne in mind that the over-all, big-scale strategy of the
Federal armies was to turn the Confederate left. The
first effective step in this direction was taken when
Forts Henry and Donelson fell, giving the Federals control of the important Cumberland and Tennessee rivers. Later the fall of Vicksburg completed the Federal
conquest of the Mississippi and cut the Confederacy in
two. But as long as the Army of Tennessee remained in
the field as an effective fighting force, the Confederate
left flank, however straitened and hard pressed, could
be maintained intact.

It was the crushing of the Army of Tennessee at the
battle of Nashville that sealed the fate of the Confederate left and of the Confederacy. After that the ultimate
outcome of the war was beyond question; it was then
merely a matter of time. On the other hand, had the
Confederates won this battle and thereafter carried

their battle flags to the banks of the Ohio River in a vigorous offensive movement, the whole aspect of the military situation would have been changed.

The Confederate commander, General John B. Hood, said that if he had been able to capture Nashville and there supply and reinforce his army, his plan was "to move into Kentucky and take position with our left at or near Richmond and our right extending toward Hazel Green, with Pound and Stony Gaps in the Cumberland Mountains at our rear. In this position I could threaten Cincinnati and recruit the army from Kentucky and Tennesse. . . . If [Sherman] returned to confront my forces or followed me directly from Georgia into Tennessee and Kentucky, I hoped then to be in condition to offer battle and, if blessed with victory, to send reinforcements to General Lee in Virginia or to march through the gaps in the Cumberland Mountains and attack Grant in rear. This latter course I would pursue in the event of defeat or of inability to offer battle to Sherman. If on the other hand he marched to join Grant, I could pass through the Cumberland gaps to Petersburg and attack Grant in rear at least two weeks before he, Sherman, could render him assistance. This move, I believed, would defeat Grant and allow General Lee, in command of our combined armies, to march upon Washington or turn upon and annihilate Sherman."[3]

It developed that this plan was impractical in the existing circumstances, and Hood's effort to put it into effect ended in failure. Some modern military experts, fortified by the priceless advantage of hindsight, have therefore felt free to describe the plan as "fantastic." It cannot be emphasized too strongly, however, that no-

[3] J. B. Hood, *Advance and Retreat* (New Orleans, 1880), 267.

body seemed to think it fantastic at the time. Grant's almost hysterical telegrams to General George H. Thomas, as Hood's threat developed, revealed a very genuine fear that this "fantastic" plan of campaign would be successful—an apprehension that was shared by Chief of Staff Henry W. Halleck, Secretary of War Edwin Stanton, and President Lincoln.

Grant was keenly aware of the dire consequences to the Federal cause if Nashville should fall, thereby freeing Hood's Army of Tennessee to operate offensively through Kentucky to the north or east. He not only did not consider Hood's plan impracticable or foredoomed to failure, but in discussing the matter after the war he attributed its failure to Hood's lack of enterprise. "If I had been in Hood's place," Grant said, "I would have gone to Louisville and on north until I came to Chicago. . . . We would have had to raise new levies. I was never so anxious during the war as at that time." [4]

General Thomas, writing in later years after mature deliberation, said of Hood's plan of campaign: "Though a failure in the end, who will say that it was not the best plan that could have been adopted by the enemy?" General James H. Wilson also said, in his memoirs written thirty years later, that Hood's movement against Nashville lacked nothing but weight to give it complete victory. [5]

A pertinent fact, likely to be overlooked in considering the situation in December, 1864, is that at this time a large proportion of the population of the Northern states was thoroughly war-weary and that both moral

[4] *Around the World with General Grant* (New York, 1879), II, 294.
[5] Van Horne, *Life of Thomas,* 251; James H. Wilson, *Under the Old Flag* (New York, Appleton-Century-Crofts, Inc., 1912), II, 16.

and financial support of the war effort were dangerously lagging. Secretary Stanton told General John M. Schofield shortly after the battle of Nashville that an early termination of the war was "an absolute financial necessity," as it had grown increasingly difficult to float the war bonds. It was obviously feared that a Confederate victory at Nashville might precipitate in the North a "peace at any price" clamor that would be irresistible.

Schofield elsewhere comments on the critical financial condition existing at the time and the importance of gaining a smashing Federal victory in the field "before the world should find out that the resources of the government had been exhausted and that the United States had not the financial strength necessary to make any further military use of men they then had on the muster and pay-rolls." He states that "the Union cause was on the very verge of failure" because it could no longer raise money; that the troops had not been paid for five months; and that Secretary Stanton had confided to the generals of the Federal army in the winter of 1864 that "the rebellion must be suppressed in the coming campaign or the effort abandoned," because the resources of the treasury were exhausted.[6]

General Wilson, who had been serving on the eastern front in Virginia just before the battle of Nashville and was familiar with the state of public opinion at that time, says that "the newspapers throughout the country were filled with prognostications of disaster. Commerce and financial affairs were disturbed. Gold was falling; the War Department was demoralized, and even General Grant himself showed greater uneasiness than he had ever exhibited before." Grant frankly acknowledged that if the South were able to prolong the war in the West into the summer of 1865, it would probably

[6] Schofield, *Forty-six Years in the Army,* 255, 315, 530.

be necessary to concede the independence of the seceded states.[7]

The culminating decisiveness of the battle of Nashville was recognized as early as 1867, when William Swinton included it in his book *The Twelve Decisive Battles of the War.* "Nashville," says Swinton, "annihilated the Confederacy in the West." General Schofield, who could never be suspected of any desire to give undue credit to Thomas, states that "The defeat and practical destruction of Hood's army in Tennessee was what paved the way to the speedy termination of the war, which the capture of Lee by Grant fully accomplished." General Isaac R. Sherwood, who was an officer in the Federal army and fought at both Franklin and Nashville, says unequivocally, "Nashville was the decisive battle of the four years' war."[8]

General John Watts duPuyster on January 4, 1876, delivered to the annual meeting of the New York Historical Society an address bearing the significant title "Nashville—the Decisive Battle of the Rebellion," in which he elaborated at some length on the subject. "Of all the battles of the great American conflict," said General duPuyster, "the most complete in its result, the finest and most perfect in its execution, strategically and tactically, the fittest as a study and as an example to be referred to and cited hereafter, was Nashville. It was the Leipsic, or better, the Waterloo of the four years' struggle. No other fight can compare with it when the forces respectively engaged are taken into consideration."

Coming down to modern times and modern critics,

[7] Wilson, *Under the Old Flag*, II, 62; *Personal Memoirs of U. S. Grant* (2d ed., New York, 1894), II, 435, 543.

[8] William Swinton, *The Twelve Decisive Battles of the War* (New York, 1867), 470; Schofield, *Forty-six Years in the Army*, 348; Gen. Isaac R. Sherwood, *Memoirs of the War* (Toledo, 1923), 149.

it is interesting to observe that General J. F. C. Fuller, in his *Decisive Battles of the U.S.A.*, published in 1942, includes Nashville along with Saratoga, Yorktown Chapultepec, Gettysburg, Santiago and the Meuse-Argonne in his account of "the battles that have decided the course of American history." In specific terms he refers to the engagement at Nashville as "that decisive battle," stating that it was Thomas' victory at Nashville and not Sherman's march through Georgia and the Carolinas that settled the war in the West and thereby decided the result of the war.[9]

The final collapse of the Southern Confederacy followed so closely after the failure of Hood's Tennessee campaign that the importance of the battle of Nashville was overshadowed and obscured by the overwhelming impact of the ending of the war and the return of the people to peaceful pursuits. The participating generals' official reports of the battle were not written until months afterwards. It was years before these reports were published, and even then they were buried in ponderous official publications which had few readers. Contemporaneously and subsequently, the battle of Nashville had less publicity and discussion than any engagement of similar proportions and importance, and this lack of publicity accounts in great degree for the general lack of appreciation of the battle's decisive significance.

General Sherman threw off the misleading aphorism that "The battle of Nashville was fought at Franklin," and this was repeated by others who wished to belittle Thomas' victory over Hood. There is, of course, no denying that the losses suffered by Hood at Franklin did so weaken him that he was a less difficult victim for

[9] Gen. J. F. C. Fuller, *Decisive Battles of the U.S.A.* (London and New York, 1942), 308 *et seq*.

Thomas at Nashville. The fact remains, however, that
the battle of Franklin, sanguinary as it was, was not
decisive in any sense of the word—except to decide that
Schofield did not feel able to stand up to the Army of
Tennessee, even on terms of approximate numerical
equality, and was glad to leave Hood in possession of
the field at Franklin as he fled to the protection of the
fortifications at Nashville.

The battle of Franklin damaged Hood and weakened
him, but by itself it would never have stopped him. In
spite of his losses there he continued to advance, and he
would have kept on advancing—into Kentucky or on
to the Ohio River or into Virginia or wherever he
wished to go—if he had not been sent reeling back in
decisive defeat by the forces of Thomas at Nashville. In
the terms of the prize ring, Franklin was a knockdown
that gave Hood a thorough shaking up and started blood
to flowing—but many badly damaged prize fighters have
got up from the canvas and gone on to win. Franklin
was a knockdown; Nashville was the knockout for
Hood.

It is impossible to question that Nashville was *a* decisive battle. An examination of all the facts, it is believed, provides inescapably convincing evidence that
it was *the* decisive battle of the war.

Table of Contents

Maps and Illustrations

THE DECISIVE BATTLE OF NASHVILLE

Prologue

THE battle of Nashville was fought on Thursday and Friday, December 15 and 16, 1864. General George H. Thomas, commanding a Federal force of about 55,000, attacked and routed the Confederate army commanded by General John B. Hood, numbering less than 25,000 in action.[1]

The battle was the climax of a long chain of military movements and developments which had begun late in 1861. At that time General Albert Sidney Johnston was sent to Tennessee by President Jefferson Davis to take command of the Department of the West. Upon assuming this command, Johnston established the front line of the Confederacy in his Department as a thinly held position stretching eastward from Columbus, Kentucky, on the Mississippi River, through Fort Henry, Fort Donelson and Bowling Green, to the Cumberland Gap in the mountains of eastern Kentucky close to the Tennessee state line. This was the Confederate frontier in

[1] It is difficult to say exactly how many men were actually engaged in the battle of Nashville—or any other battle. The army returns use such loose and confusing designations as "aggregate present," "effective present," "present for duty," "present for duty, equipped," etc. The official returns of the Army of Tennessee on December 10, 1864, showed Hood's total "present effective" infantry, cavalry, and artillery to be 23,053, which seems to be consistent with the strength reported on November 6, 30,600. Thomas' returns on December 10, 1864, show a total of 71,842 "present for duty, equipped." This, however, included a number of reserve and unassigned troops. The forces actually taking part in the fighting of the battle of Nashville are listed as: Wood's Corps, 14,171; Schofield's, 10,207; Smith's, 10,461; Steedman's, 7,541; Wilson's, 12,500—a total of 54,881.

the West—the left flank of the Confederacy, militarily speaking.

The fall of Fort Donelson on the Cumberland River in February, 1862, rendered this line untenable, and Johnston ordered a general retreat, abandoning Nashville to the enemy. Johnston fell back from Nashville to Corinth, Mississippi, where he gathered all the available Confederate troops and early in April launched a savage surprise attack on the Federal forces under General Ulysses S. Grant at Shiloh in western Tennessee. Johnston was killed the first day of that battle and was succeeded by General P. G. T. Beauregard, who, after a second day of inconclusive fighting, retreated to Corinth and later to Tupelo, Mississippi. Beauregard was soon replaced by General Braxton Bragg, who led a brilliant but fruitless invasion of Kentucky late in the year, fighting the useless battle of Perryville and then retreating unmolested into Tennessee. Here Bragg concentrated his forces at Murfreesboro, where he remained until General William S. Rosecrans moved out from Nashville and engaged him in two days of fighting, beginning December 31, 1862—another furious and gory but indecisive battle, from which Bragg retired unpursued.

After several months of inactivity on both sides, Rosecrans went into action in June, 1863, and soon maneuvered Bragg all the way to Chattanooga in a series of strategic moves involving relatively little actual fighting but achieving great results. Bragg later moved out of Chattanooga to meet Rosecrans in northern Georgia, where he fought and won the battle of Chickamauga, only to lose the effects of that victory by fighting and losing the battle of Missionary Ridge. Bragg was succeeded as commander of the army by Joseph E. Johnston, who was in command at Dalton, Georgia, when Sherman moved against him in May, 1864. General

Johnston's effort to draw the Federals into an unfavorable position in Georgia by means of a skillful retreat did not please the impatient President Davis, who did not like Johnston very much in any case. Accordingly Johnston was displaced in July, 1864, and the command given to General John Bell Hood, who had been commanding a corps in Johnston's army.

Hood was a young man, only 31 years old, when he assumed command of the Army of Tennessee with the provisional rank of a full general. He had been graduated from West Point in 1853 and had served in Texas with the celebrated Second Cavalry regiment of which Albert Sidney Johnston was colonel and R. E. Lee lieutenant colonel, with George H. Thomas and William J. Hardee serving as majors. He resigned his commission in 1861 and was soon in the midst of the fighting in Virginia, as colonel of a regiment of Texans. He quickly advanced to the command of a brigade and then a division, and by his headlong gallantry and effective leadership attracted the admiring attention of both Lee and Stonewall Jackson. At Gettysburg a bullet shattered his left arm, and he never regained the use of it. At Chickamauga, where he led his division in the charge that broke through and started the rout of the Federal forces, he suffered a wound in his right leg which necessitated its removal at the hip. During his convalescence in Richmond he became a sort of protégé of Jefferson Davis, and as soon as he was able to resume active service he was sent to the Army of Tennessee as a corps commander. When he succeeded to the command of that army, there were many who shared Bragg's cautiously expressed opinion that Hood was "not a genius, not a great general." There was also serious apprehension as to the physical efficiency of an army commander who carried one arm in a sling and used a crutch as a necessary aid in walking. But President Davis had great confidence in the young hero of Gettysburg and Chickamauga and promoted him in preference to General Hardee, despite advice to the contrary.

General Hood accepted command of the Army of Tennessee with a clear understanding that his appointment constituted a virtual mandate to discontinue his predecessor's Fabian tactics and to engage Sherman in active combat. So there ensued the battles around Atlanta, resulting in heavy casualties on both sides and the loss of that city to the Federals. Undismayed by this disaster, however, Hood made a sudden and unexpected movement against Sherman's line of supply, attacking the railroad north of Atlanta and forcing Sherman out of Atlanta in pursuit. Within a few days the armies were back in the neighborhood of Dalton, where the campaign had started in May. Hood then bounded off into northeastern Alabama, followed warily by Sherman, neither commander seeming eager to precipitate a battle.

It was at this juncture that General Hood decided on the bold Tennessee campaign which might have exerted such a different influence on the outcome of the war if it had been successful. It is trite to say that nothing succeeds like success, but Hood's Tennessee campaign is a striking example of the truth of this old saying. His campaign failed, so it has been easy to leap to the conclusion that failure was inevitable and to label Hood conventionally as an incompetent bungler. But failure was not inevitable or foreordained. On the contrary, if Hood had been able to move with just a little more celerity, if on just one or two occasions Fortune's balance had tilted in his favor instead of against him, his daringly conceived plan might well have succeeded. And then perhaps the little village of Appomattox

Court House might have slept on forever in its dusty obscurity.

Hood's plan, which was approved by his then superior commanding officer, General Beauregard, and also given tacit approval by President Davis, was to make a sudden turn and march northward in a quick dash across northern Alabama into Middle Tennessee. If able to move swiftly enough, he considered it militarily feasible to overpower whatever forces might be hastily gathered to protect Nashville and regain possession of that important center and its vast store of supplies. Then, with no other organized Federal army of importance in front of him, he could move on into Kentucky, threatening Louisville and Cincinnati and definitely transferring the initiative and offensive to the side of the Confederates.

Sherman was momentarily bewildered by the sudden and unexpected shift in his adversary's strategy, but he was himself nursing an equally daring and unorthodox idea which Hood's movement now enabled him to put into effect. For some time he had been considering the desirability of staging a punitive and destructive march to the sea, designed to "make Georgia howl,"[2] and this withdrawal of Hood from his front cleared the way for this movement.

"Hood is not going to enter Tennessee,"[3] Sherman assured Grant in the most positive terms, but Grant would not give his consent to the march to the sea until Sherman reassured him by promising to leave General Thomas in charge of the defense of Tennessee and to assign to Thomas sufficient force to enable him to offer

[2] *The War of the Rebellion, a Compilation of the Official Records of the Union and Confederate Armies* (Washington, 1880-1901), Ser. I, Vol. XXXIX, Pt. III, 162 (hereinafter referred to as *Official Records;* all citations are to Series I).

[3] Van Horne, *Life of Thomas,* 256.

effective resistance to Hood's advance. Sherman had such an overwhelmingly superior force that he was able to assign a part of it to Thomas and still leave himself an army of 60,000 seasoned veterans to conduct the virtually unopposed march through Georgia.

George Henry Thomas was the oldest general officer involved in the Nashville campaign, having been born in Virginia in 1816. In 1840 he had been graduated from West Point, where he was a roommate of William Tecumseh Sherman. After fighting the Indians in Florida and serving efficiently in the Mexican War, he was back at West Point in 1853 as artillery instructor, John B. Hood and John M. Schofield being among the cadets at that time. When Virginia seceded in 1861, Thomas, unlike R. E. Lee, considered that his loyalty to the United States took precedence over his loyalty to Virginia and remained in the old Army. Lee and Johnston having gone with the Confederacy, Thomas was promptly advanced to the rank of colonel of the Second Cavalry and in August, 1861, was made a briga-dier general. He fought and won the battle of Mill Springs or Fishing Creek (Kentucky) in January, 1862; but, accompanying Buell, his division reached Shiloh after that battle was over. He served with notable dis-tinction at Perryville, Murfreesboro, and Chickamauga, where his division was the last to leave the field, earning for him the name "The Rock of Chickamauga." In Oc-tober, 1863, he was put in charge of the Department and the Army of the Cumberland,[4] and at Missionary Ridge

[4] The Federal armies bore names relating to the rivers near which they originally operated: the Army of the Cumberland, the Army of the Tennessee, the Army of the Potomac, etc. The names of the Con-federate armies related to the state or locality in which they principally fought: the Army of Tennessee, the Army of Northern Virginia. The North and South also followed different systems in identifying their

it was his command that broke the Confederate defenses and gave the Federal forces the victory. His Army of the Cumberland occupied the center in Sherman's advance into Georgia in the spring of 1864, and in this campaign Sherman learned at close quarters the military skill and dependability of his one-time roommate.

The headquarters of the Department of the Cumberland was at Nashville, and Thomas had returned to that city following the fall of Atlanta to look after the affairs of his department. He maintained his military offices in the Cunningham residence on High Street (now Sixth Avenue North),[5] but lived at the St. Cloud Hotel on the corner of Church and Summer (now Fifth Avenue). Thomas was the obvious and natural choice for command of the defenses of Tennessee, and Sherman knew he was leaving this important assignment in capable hands.

Thomas' first request, when ordered to assume charge of the defense against Hood's advance, was that his own Fourteenth Corps be sent to Nashville to serve him

---

corps, divisions, and brigades. In the Federal armies the numerical system was followed; for example, the groups of regiments commanded by Colonel P. Sidney Post at Nashville was officially the Second Brigade of the Third Division of the Fourth Army Corps. The Confederate corps, divisions, and brigades were known by the names of their commanders: Cheatham's Corps; Bate's Division; Jackson's Brigade. This was sometimes confusing, for when commanding officers were killed or were promoted, the outfits (particularly the divisions and brigades) tended to retain the names of their original commanders. For instance, the division originally commanded by General B. F. Cheatham was still known as "Cheatham's Division" even after he had been made a corps commander and was succeeded in command of the division by General John C. Brown. Brown was wounded at Franklin and the command fell on General Mark P. Lowrey, so this body of troops was variously known as Cheatham's, Brown's, or Lowrey's Division.

[5] The site of the house is now marked by a plaque placed by the Tennessee Historical Commission.

there. Sherman, however, declined, saying, "It is too compact and reliable a corps for me to leave behind."[6] Sherman did order the Fourth Corps, 12,000 men under General David S. Stanley, to report to Thomas at Nashville; in addition, a number of new regiments, all the returning convalescents, and other incidental reinforcements were directed to Nashville to help build up a formidable force there. Thomas' command, of course, included the garrisons stationed at Nashville, Chattanooga, and other strategic points, as well as the detachments of men in the blockhouses along the railroads. In addition, two divisions of veteran troops under General Andrew Jackson Smith, then serving in Missouri, were ordered to Nashville.

Smith was a West Pointer, nearly fifty years old, and had been described by Sherman as a man who "will fight all the time." He had seen service in the Mexican War and on the Western frontier and had served in various campaigns in Mississppi and Louisiana. His principal claim to military distinction lay in the fact that in the summer of 1864 he commanded the Federal force at Harrisburg, Mississippi, which successfully repelled the Confederate attack under the nominal command of Nathan Bedford Forrest. Smith lost no time in retreating from Harrisburg after the fight there, but he was pridefully pointed out as the man who had "whipped Forrest"—a rare distinction among Federal leaders. Smith was a dogged fighter of considerable ability, and his command consisted of a seasoned lot of well-trained veteran fighters. His accession lent much valuable strength to Thomas' defensive force.

Owing to transportation difficulties, Smith was delayed in moving from Missouri; but Stanley got under way at once, proceeding by rail to Tullahoma and

6 Van Horne, *Life of Thomas*, 261.

marching from there to Pulaski, seventy-three miles south of Nashville. A few days later General John M. Schofield, with the Twenty-third Corps of 10,000 men, was also sent back by Sherman, with orders to follow Stanley to Tullahoma and thence to Pulaski. Schofield had hardly started, however, before Forrest made his spectacular raid against Johnsonville, an important rail-head on the Tennessee River about seventy miles west of Nashville, and Thomas ordered Schofield to proceed by rail directly to Nashville and thence with a part of his troops to Johnsonville. Forrest had finished his work and gone, however, when Schofield arrived there, so he and his men retraced their steps to Nashville and thence to the neighborhood of Pulaski, arriving on November 13. Here he combined his corps with that of General Stanley, assuming command of the total force of 22,000 men by virtue of his rank as a department commander.

Schofield, a young West Pointer, had just passed his thirty-third birthday. At the academy he had been a classmate of Hood's, and remembered him as "a jolly good fellow" who had some difficulty in keeping up with his classes. Schofield's career at the academy was full of ups and downs, and one year he had 196 demerits out of a possible 200. At one time he narrowly escaped dismissal, but he stood at the head of his class in tactics when he graduated in 1853. During the early days of the war he served in Missouri, but early in 1864 he was given command of the Department and Army of the Ohio. In May of 1864 the Army of the Ohio, designated the Twenty-third Corps, became a part of Sherman's force assembled for the advance into Georgia, and he served under Sherman until the capture of Atlanta.

The only cavalry immediately available to Thomas consisted of the two mounted divisions of General John

T. Croxton and General Edward Hatch. Sherman had taken the cream of the Federal cavalry with him on his march through Georgia, having sent all the unmounted troopers back to Nashville and to Louisville to serve under Thomas when and if they could be remounted. General James H. Wilson, who had been serving with the Federal cavalry in Virginia had just been assigned to Sherman to act as the chief of the mounted forces in Sherman's military division. He was ordered to report to Thomas to assist him in the defense of Tennessee, but he did not reach the scene of his new duties and take command until late in October. Meanwhile Croxton and Hatch were detailed to patrol the Tennessee River and if possible prevent Hood's crossing, but their force was totally inadequate to any such assignment.

Hood also was having cavalry trouble. One of the conditions imposed on him by Beauregard in authorizing the present movement was that he must leave the bulk of Wheeler's cavalry south of the Tennessee River, taking with him only two brigades under General William Hicks Jackson. Forrest, Hood was told, would be ordered to join him when he crossed the river and would serve under him on his northward march. Forrest at the time was engaged in his raid into West Tennessee which culminated in his destructive swoop onto Johnsonville. As soon as he received his orders, however, he abandoned these activities and made his way with his troopers and his artillery to the Tuscumbia-Sheffield crossing point, where he reported to Hood on November 14.

Nathan Bedford Forrest was not a graduate of any military school; in fact he had had very little formal education of any kind. At the time of the secession of Tennessee he was forty years old, a successful and wealthy businessman in Memphis. He promptly offered his services to his state and proceeded to organize a regiment of cavalry at his own expense. His advancement in rank was rapid, as his native energy, good judgment, and common sense, coupled with an apparently instinctive genius for military strategy and tactics, soon made it obvious that he was a cavalry commander of transcendent ability. At the time he reported to Hood he was at the peak of his career, probably the most brilliant and capable cavalry leader in the Confederate service. He was to prove a tower of strength to Hood in his advance and retreat, although he and his men were not used to their maximum possibilities in the actual fighting at Nashville.

From the first the movement of Hood's army, difficult at best and dependent for success on speed and celerity, had encountered obstacles. Crossing the Tennessee River at Guntersville, in northeastern Alabama, as originally planned, had been found to be impracticable, and so the men were forced to trudge on across the state to Tuscumbia to cross the river. Arriving there on October 30, Hood had suffered his first disappointment: supplies which he was expecting to find there had not arrived, and the rebuilding of the railroad from Corinth to Tuscumbia had not been completed. Then came heavy rains, making it difficult to move the wagons. A pontoon bridge had to be built across the Tennessee. All in all, three precious weeks were spent there—weeks that Hood could not afford to lose, weeks that were of supremely vital value to Thomas in building up his defensive force. At length on November 20, with the rain still falling and the roads hub-deep in mud, the Confederates began to move northward. Forrest's mounted men fanned out in the van of the infantry, as Croxton and Hatch reported the crossing and retired skirmishing.

Hood's effective force when he crossed the Tennessee and started in the direction of Nashville amounted to less than 40,000 men—about 8,000 cavalry and 30,000 infantry. The infantry force was divided into three army corps, commanded by Generals Cheatham, Stewart, and Lee.

Benjamin Franklin Cheatham was the oldest of Hood's corps commanders, having been born in Nashville on October 20, 1820. He had served as a colonel of Tennessee volunteer infantry in the Mexican War, and was later a major general of the state militia. When Tennessee seceded and joined the Southern Confederacy, Cheatham was made a brigadier general in the Confederate Provisional Army and was advanced to the rank of major general in March, 1862. He served with the Army of Tennessee through all its engagements, from Shiloh to the end of the war. When General Hardee, unable to reconcile himself to serving under Hood, asked to be transferred to some other command after the battles around Atlanta, Cheatham was given command of Hardee's old corps and advanced to the duty of lieutenant general. He was sometimes at loggerheads with his superior officers, but he had the reputation of being a hard fighter and was highly regarded by the men who served under him.

Alexander Peter Stewart was a native Tennessean, born in 1821. He was graduated from West Point in 1842, but he resigned his commission in 1845, and from then until the secession of Tennessee in 1861 he served on the faculties of the University of Nashville and Cumberland University, at Lebanon, Tennessee. He was given a brigadier general's commission in the Confederate army in November, 1861, and given command of a brigade under General Leonidas Polk in the

Army of Tennessee. He was promoted to the rank of major general in June, 1863, and when Polk was killed in June, 1864, he was given the command of Polk's corps with the temporary rank of lieutenant general. Stephen Dill Lee was the youngest corps commander in the Army of Tennessee—indeed, was the youngest lieutenant general in the whole Confederate army, having been born in Charleston, South Carolina, in 1833 and graduated from West Point in 1854. Despite his youth, however, he had a record for length of service to the Confederacy which was equaled by few and surpassed by none; he also had the unusual distinction of having served as a commanding general officer in all branches of the service. He had volunteered his services to his state when South Carolina seceded in December, 1860, and had become an aide on the staff of General Beauregard. In this capacity he personally delivered the Confederate ultimatum to Major Robert Anderson in Fort Sumter on April 11, 1861, and the next day gave the order to his own artillery which opened the bombardment on the fort and started the war. Later he served as an artillery officer with the Army of Northern Virginia, and Hood had good reason to remember gratefully the effective support of Lee's guns at Sharpsburg when Hood's division was hard pressed there. When, after Sharpsburg, President Davis asked R. E. Lee to select his most efficient artillery officer for duty as commander of the Confederate artillery in Mississippi, Stephen D. Lee was recommended for this promotion and in November, 1862, was sent to Vicksburg with the rank of brigadier general. Here he served until Pemberton's surrender of the city on July 4, 1863; he was exchanged in August and was promoted to major general and put in command of all the cavalry in Mississippi, Alabama, West Tennessee, and Louisiana. When Hood was given command of the Army of Tennessee before Atlanta, Lee was assigned to the command of Hood's corps, with the rank of lieutenant general.

As Hood's army started its march northward after crossing the Tennessee, Schofield, at Pulaski, was watchful. When it became clear that the movement of the Confederates was turning his flank, he moved back rapidly toward Columbia, on the south bank of Duck River, forty-three miles south of Nashville, where he arrived on November 24 and took up a strong defensive position. Hood reached Columbia on November 26 and formed a line of battle and demonstrated against Schofield, who prudently retired to the north bank of the Duck the following night.

Then on November 29 Hood began an elaborately designed movement by means of which he hoped to trap Schofield into battle under fatally disadvantageous circumstances. Leaving Lee's corps on the south bank of the river at Columbia to occupy Schofield's attention with artillery demonstrations, Hood with his other two infantry corps crossed the river a few miles east of Columbia. His plan was to make a wide sweep around Schofield's left flank and come back into the Columbia-Nashville highway at Spring Hill, twelve miles in the Federals' rear, and there destroy or severely cripple them. Forrest crossed ahead of the infantry and had little trouble in sweeping the Federal cavalry out of the way, as the infantry advanced.

General Wilson was now in personal charge of the mounted forces assigned to Schofield's assistance. Wilson was a brash and self-assertive young West Pointer, just twenty-seven years old, with great confidence in his own ability. He had been serving with the Federal cavalry in Virginia, where he had attracted the favorable attention of Sheridan and Grant. He later showed great energy and ability in leading the greatly expanded and well-equipped cavalry force under his command, but in this initial clash with Forrest he was clearly overmatched and outgeneraled.

The first phases of Hood's flanking maneuver were carried off smoothly enough. Having brushed Wilson aside, Forrest arrived in the neighborhood of Spring Hill early in the afternoon, and the leading detachments of the Confederate infantry reached the outskirts of the little town long before nightfall. But Schofield had not been idle. Recognizing the strategic importance of Spring Hill, he had marched one of his divisions to that point early in the day, taking advantage of the shorter distance and better marching conditions afforded by the macadamized highway. This movement was handled with promptness and efficiency, and the Federal division with its artillery was entrenched there in a strong defensive position when Hood's advancing forces began to arrive.

Orders were quickly given by Hood that the Federals be attacked and the road seized, but here ensued one of the still unexplained mysteries of the war. After a little fitful and ineffective skirmishing, there developed an inexplicable confusion and infirmity in the Confederate command. As a result of this mysterious paralysis of purpose, accentuated by the coming of darkness on the short November day, all the Confederate troops' movements were halted and they bivouacked for the night in sight of the all-important road but not in possession of it. Schofield, now thoroughly aroused to the perilous nature of his situation, hurried his whole army during the night along the road through Spring Hill in the direction of Nashville, unimpeded by the nearby but strangely inert Confederates.[7]

When Hood awoke on the morning of November 30 and found that his quarry had escaped the carefully planned trap, he was enraged. Angrily berating his subordinates, he lashed his army into a double-quick pursuit of the fleeing Federals. Schofield, with several hours' lead, arrived at Franklin early in the morning, fully expecting to have his men and wagons across the Harpeth River there by noon and continue on to Nashville as ordered. Finding the highway bridge across the river destroyed, his engineers went to work to patch it into usable condition and to plank the railroad bridge so it could be used for the passage of the wagon train. Meanwhile the troops, infantry and artillery, were placed in strongly fortified entrenchments on the southern outskirts of the little town, and Schofield telegraphed Thomas of his plight, asking for reinforcements. Thomas could not send him any help; on the contrary, he asked him if he could "hold Hood at Franklin for three days or longer."[8] Schofield, who was decidedly jittery, suggested retiring to Brentwood, about seven miles from Nashville, there to meet reinforcements to be sent out by Thomas. He expressed the fear that in his present position he would be flanked by Forrest, commenting disgustedly, "Wilson is entirely unable to cope with him."[9] But Thomas had no reinforcements to send him, and so Schofield held his men

---

[7] Various explanations have been advanced for the Confederate fiasco at Spring Hill. Whatever the neglect or ineptitude of any of his subordinates, however, the responsibility rests on Hood. He was the commander of the Army; it was his duty to give the orders appropriate to the conditions as he found them—and to see that his orders were carried out.

[8] Schofield, *Forty-six Years in the Army,* 263.

[9] *Ibid.,* 222.

in their breastworks at Franklin, hoping that Hood, when he arrived, would not be rash enough to attack.

When the pursuing Confederate forces reached Franklin late in the afternoon, Hood, apparently unaware of or unimpressed by the great strength of the enemy's position, ordered an immediate frontal assault on the Federal lines. This was in direct disregard of the advice of Forrest, who, having reconnoitered the Federal position, said that with his mounted men and one division of infantry he could cross the Harpeth above the town and get in the Federal rear. But Hood, consumed with a raging impatience for combat, was determined to attack and attack right now, using the force then present. This available force consisted only of the two corps commanded by Stewart and Cheatham, together with two pieces of artillery. Lee's corps, accompanied by the main body of the artillery and the wagon train, were hurrying up from Columbia, where they had been left, but were still far in the rear.

The gallantry and tenacious persistence of the Confederate attack at Franklin was unexcelled in the whole history of the war, but it was unsuccessful—indeed, almost disastrous. The Confederates suffered a loss of more than 6,000 killed, wounded, and missing, including a phenomenally heavy toll of officers. The Federals, fighting behind breastworks, suffered serious but not severe losses, General Stanley being one of the wounded. The fighting continued intermittently from about 4 P.M. into the night, but by about 9 o'clock the exhausted Confederates ceased firing. Schofield retreated during the night to the safety of the fortifications of Nashville, leaving his dead and wounded on the battlefield, which was abandoned to the Confederates. "To remain longer at Franklin was to seriously hazard the loss of my army," Schofield later reported to

Thomas. "I had found it impossible to detain him [Hood] long enough to get re-enforcements at Franklin."[10]

Schofield's urgent appeals for help were ineffective for the simple reason that Thomas at that time had no immediately available force which could be sent to his relief. The steamboats carrying Smith and his two divisions did not begin to arrive in Nashville until the very day the battle was fought at Franklin, and were not all up until December 2. Other reinforcements were on the way to Nashville, but they could not be diverted to Schofield's aid. General James B. Steedman, with a provisional division of 5,000 men and two brigades of colored troops, were in process of being brought up from Chattanooga to Nashville, where they arrived on the evening of December 1. On November 29 Thomas had ordered General Milroy and his Tullahoma garrison to reinforce General Lovell H. Rousseau at Murfreesboro, which was being flanked by Hood's advance, and they were en route on the thirtieth but beyond the possibility of being sent to Schofield's assistance. As had been true at Shiloh, the Federal forces seemed by providential timing to arrive at Nashville in the nick of time.

As matters stood on the morning of December 1, Hood found himself in possession of the Franklin battlefield, with his preceding day's opponent in precipitate flight. Hood might claim a technical victory, but he knew very well as he looked at the thousands of dead and wounded on the field that he could not stand any more such victories. His immediate problem was to bury the dead of both sides and give such medical attention as was possible to the wounded. Having done that, he must answer for himself the vital and vexing question, What to do next?

[10] *Official Records*, Vol. XLV, Pt. I, 344.

There were several possible procedures open to the Confederate commander. He could acknowledge frankly that he had been outmaneuvered, although not outfought, admit that his Tennessee campaign was a failure, and retreat with his surviving army intact, to fight another day. This might have been the most prudent thing to do, especially in view of what is known now of the then-existing circumstances. Aside, however, from the unfavorable psychological effect on his troops of such a backward step, to a leader of Hood's combative temperament a retreat was unthinkable. A more artful strategist might have moved quickly with his whole force to Murfreesboro, overpowered its garrison, entrenched himself there, and restored the *status quo* of late 1862. If determined to continued on the aggressive, he might have attempted to force a crossing of the Cumberland River above Nashville and by this movement threaten the Federal communications. This was suggested by some of Hood's advisors, but he did not view such strategy with favor. One other desperate possibility, of course, was to advance on Nashville at once and launch a direct assault on the fortifications of the city; but in the absence of information as to the nature of the city's defenses and defending force, even Hood was not inclined to risk such an effort.

What Hood finally decided to do was move his army to a position on the hills south of Nashville, entrench and maintain himself in a defensive and threatening attitude there, and wait for General Thomas to make the next move. In later years he carefully explained and justified this perilous policy, but his explanation is thoroughly unconvincing:

"After the failure of my cherished plan to crush Schofield's army before it reached its strongly fortified position around Nashville, I remained with an effective force of only twenty-three thousand and fifty-three (23,053). I was therefore well aware of our inability to attack the Federals in their new stronghold with any hope of success, although Schofield's troops had abandoned the field at Franklin, leaving their dead and wounded in our possession, and had hastened with considerable alarm into their fortifications—which latter information, in regard to their condition after the battle, I obtained through spies. I knew equally well that in the absence of the prestige of complete victory I could not venture with my small force to cross the Cumberland River into Kentucky without first receiving reinforcements from the Trans-Mississippi Department. I felt convinced that the Tennesseans and Kentuckians would not join our forces, since we had failed in the first instance to defeat the Federal army and capture Nashville. The President was still urgent in his instructions relative to the transference of troops to the Army of Tennessee from Texas, and I daily hoped to receive the glad tidings of their safe passage across the Mississippi River.

"Thus, unless strengthened by these long looked for reinforcements, the only remaining chance of success in the campaign at this juncture was to take position, entrench around Nashville and await Thomas's attack which, if handsomely repulsed, might afford us an opportunity to follow up our advantage on the spot and enter the city on the heels of the enemy.

"I could not afford to turn southward, unless for the special purpose of forming a junction with the expected reinforcements from Texas, and with the avowed intention to march back again upon Nashville. In truth, our army was then in that condition which rendered it more judicious the men should face a decisive issue rather than retreat—in other words, rather than re-

nounce the honor of their cause, without having made a
last and manful effort to lift up the sinking fortunes
of the Confederacy.

"I therefore determined to move upon Nashville, to
entrench, to accept the chances of reinforcements from
Texas, and even at the risk of an attack in the meantime
by overwhelming numbers, to adopt the only feasible
means of defeating the enemy with my reduced numbers, viz., to await his attack and, if favored by success,
to follow him into his works. I was apprised of each accession to Thomas's army, but was still unwilling to
abandon the ground as long as I saw a shadow of probability of assistance from the Trans-Mississippi Department or of victory in battle; and, as I have just remarked, the troops would, I believed, return better
satisfied even after defeat if, in grasping at the last
straw, they felt that a brave and vigorous effort had been
made to save the country from disaster. Such at the
time was my opinion, which I have since had no reason
to alter." [11]

There is an old military maxim, credited to Napoleon, to the effect that "The passive defensive is a
form of deferred suicide." Perhaps Hood was not familiar with this maxim; at any rate, he was not guided
by it. But the next two weeks were to prove that Napoleon was right.

[11] Hood, *Advance and Retreat*, 299.

The Stronghold Invested

As General Hood undoubtedly knew, for his spies sifted freely into and out of the city, Nashville was a strongly defended place—probably the most thoroughly and skillfully fortified city on the American continent at that time. A city of about 30,000 inhabitants in 1861, its population had swelled to around 100,000 since the Federal occupation in February, 1862. It had become a center of communication, transportation, and supply for the Federal military activities in the Western theater, and immense stores of supplies were accumulated here. The protection of the city from capture by the Confederates was recognized as a matter of major importance.

Soon after the Federal occupation of the city Captain James St. Clair Morton of the Corps of Engineers of the United States Army was ordered by General Don Carlos Buell to go to Nashville and select sites for redoubts to protect the city. "For the present," Buell said, "I only propose to throw up small works to hold from four to six companies and from two to four pieces of artillery. They should be in the edge of the city, to command the principal thoroughfares and other prominent points. . . . See Governor [Andrew] Johnson, and if he approves, devise some defenses also around the capitol; devise also some defenses for the bridge."[1]

Captain Morton was a capable Army engineer, having served as professor of engineering at West Point, of

1 *Official Records*, Vol. XVI, Pt. II, 268.

which he was a graduate. After surveying the situation at Nashville he devised a defensive system based on three large forts: Fort Negley, on St. Cloud Hill; Fort Morton (named for himself), across the Franklin pike to the northwest on the high hill just south of South Street, where the city now maintains a rock quarry; and Fort Houston, on the rising ground where Division Street now intersects Sixteenth Avenue South.

The home of Russell Houston, a well-to-do Union sympathizer, was located on this third hill, and his loyalty was rewarded by having his home torn down to make way for the fort. As a sop to his feelings, the fort was named for him; but later on he lost even that distinction, when the name of the fortification was changed to Fort McCook in honor of General Dan McCook of the Federal army. A marker designating this spot is now to be seen in the lawn of the filling station located where the fort formerly stood.

Morton also planned a blockhouse on Casino Hill, west of Fort Negley and south of Fort Morton (where the city reservoir now stands), his idea being that the guns of Negley and Morton would control Casino. In deference to Andrew Johnson's forcibly expressed fears of raiding rebels, Morton built some earth parapets and cedar log stockades around the Capitol. These were supplemented by breastworks made of cotton bales, manned with a regiment of infantry and mounting fifteen guns; and the military governor felt a little more secure.

George D. Prentice, the fire-eating pro-Union editor of the Louisville Courier, was at this time trying to turn a more or less honest penny by speculating in cotton, and he had just invested $5,000 in this commodity in Nashville. When his precious bales were seized and used in the Capitol's fortifications, he wrote a plaintive letter to Governor Johnson, bewailing the fact that less expensive material for fortifications could not be found—apparently, with no results.

Forts Morton and Houston were planned as very large permanent works with detached stone scarps. They were expected to be strong enough to hold out even if the city was captured by an attacking army, and therefore they were built large enough to store the defensive materials and provisions needed to resist a siege, in the event that the lines around the city could not be maintained.

St. Cloud Hill, the site selected for Fort Negley, had been a popular picnic ground for the citizens of Nashville before the war, its slopes being covered with a grove of oak trees. But the beautiful grove was laid low by the axes of the 2,000 impressed slaves put to work on the fortification there; and the nearby Asylum for the Blind, only recently erected at a cost of $40,000, was blown up and destroyed to make way for the play of the guns to be placed in the fort. The fort derived its name from General James S. Negley of Pennsylvania, who had been left in command of the Nashville garrison late in the summer of 1862 when Buell went off to fight Bragg in Kentucky. Following the Battle of Chickamauga, however, the fame of General Negley became slightly tarnished, when he was censured for his conduct in the battle and relieved of his command by General William S. Rosecrans. In 1865, then, Fort Negley became offically Fort Harker, although it has always been known locally by its original name.

Work on these main fortifications progressed on a large but slow scale until November, 1864, when Hood's march into Tennessee necessitated the quick concentration of the greatest possible defensive force in Nashville. General Zealous B. Tower of the Army Engineers was thereupon placed in charge of the work and not only pushed forward the completion of the forts already begun by Captain Morton but in addition started to work feverishly on a number of additional forts designed to sustain an entrenched line all around the city.

Under General Tower's direction, a large battery of two bastion fronts for fifteen guns, supported by rifle pits, was placed on what was officially called Hill 210, located in North Nashville, near the corner of Twenty-third Avenue North and Hermosa Street, where the Washington Junior High School is now located.

On the hill just south of Jefferson Street, where Jubilee Hall of Fisk University now stands, was built Fort Gillem (later called Fort Sill), named in honor of General Alvin C. Gillem, who had charge of the construction of the fort while commander of the Tenth Tennessee (Federal) Regiment. It was a redoubt about a hundred and twenty feet square, with narrow ditches, walled with dry stone walls six feet high, with embrasures for thirteen guns, two service magazines, and a blockhouse keep.

The next link in the chain of fortifications to the northward was Fort Garesché, named for Colonel Julius P. Garesché, who had been killed at the battle of Murfreesboro. It was built by the Second Ohio Volunteers on the knoll crossed by the old Hyde's Ferry road (now Buchanan Street) about at the intersection of that street with the present Twenty-fifth and Twenty-sixth avenues —about a mile north of Fort Gillem and three fourths of a mile from the ferry. This position had a good command over the approaches in every direction, mounted fourteen guns, and had three magazines.

A redoubt called Battery Donaldson, named for General J. L. Donaldson (later called Fort W. D. Whipple), was situated midway between Forts Gillem and Garesché. This was a small battery with seven embrasures and a bomb-proof octagonal blockhouse with ten-foot sides.[2]

As Hood drew near to Nashville, General Tower took charge of all the men of the quartermaster and railroad departments, together with impressed slaves and citizens of Nashville, and all hands were put to work constructing a strong double line of breastworks which would connect these forts and provide continuous inner and outer lines of defense around the city. The Cumberland River, patrolled by gunboats, constituted an effective protection on one side, and the entrenched lines followed a roughly circular course beginning at the eminence on the bank of the river above the city at the present site of the City Hospital and ending on the hill where the Tennessee Agricultural and Industrial State University now stands, overlooking the river. These lines crossed and effectively commanded the eight principal roads leading out of the city like the spokes of a wheel: from east to west, the Lebanon, Murfreesboro, Nolensville, Franklin, Granny White, Hillsboro, Harding, and Charlotte turnpikes.[3]

The geographical location of Nashville, in a big bend

2 *Ibid.*, Vol. XLIX, Pt. II, 775-82.

3 In detail, the Federal line of defenses commenced at the hill then occupied by the city reservoir, now the site of the City Hospital, and ran through South Nashville, across the campus of the old University of Nashville (where the Children's Museum and Howard School are now located) and just north of the City Cemetery to Forts Negley, Morton, and Casino. From Fort Morton the interior line went in a diagonal, generally northwesterly direction to a horseshoe-shaped salient located on the highest part of the present campus of Vanderbilt University, which was then a part of the Taylor farm. A remnant of this earthwork, where a battery was mounted, can still be seen in the yard of the residence formerly occupied by Chancellor Kirkland to the west of Vanderbilt Hospital, then the location of the Taylor barn. From this point the interior line continued northward through the present Vanderbilt campus across West End Avenue, about as Twenty-

of the river, naturally made the river and its protection a large factor in the defense of the city, and General Thomas co-operated closely with the naval officers in charge of the Federal gunboats stationed on the river, both above and below the city.

---

third Avenue now runs, to the rear of the Elliston home place, where the Father Ryan High School now stands, and on across the Nashville and Chattanooga railroad track to Hill 210 in North Nashville, where the Washington Junior High School now stands. From Hill 210 the line went on to Fort Gillem, present site of Fisk University, thence by Battery Donaldson to Fort Garesché, near Hyde's Ferry on the river. This entrenchment, seven miles long, was supported by twenty batteries of heavy guns and completely enclosed the hospitals and stores of Nashville.

This, however, was only the interior line of defense; the exterior line was considerably in advance of this interior position. On the left the advanced line just about coincided with the interior works in that sector from the river to Fort Casino. From Casino the outer line went in a southwesterly direction, along the tops of the high hills east of the Granny White pike, crossing that pike just beyond where it is now intersected by Acklen Avenue and continuing on up and over the rocky hill to the west of the pike where the Lawrence home stood. The breastworks, still to be seen, ran close by the front door of the house, which was occupied as headquarters by General Samuel Beatty and his staff. From this point the line followed the high ground westward across the Acklen farm, south of the present campus of Belmont College. The Acklen mansion, now the main building of the Belmont group, was the headquarters of General Thomas J. Wood; and the tall brick tower still standing on the college campus was used by the Federal soldiers as an observation post. (Before the battle started, at the thoughtful suggestion of General Wood, the art treasures of the Acklen home—its paintings, statuary, and other valuables—were carried into town and stored temporarily in the residence of Mrs. James K. Polk, the widow of the President.) From the Acklen grounds, crossing the present Belmont Boulevard at about Blair Boulevard, Thomas' line went westward on to the high hill between Belmont and the Hillsboro pike, and on the top of this hill was located the Federal main salient and battery, the pivot of the turning movement of the Federal army when the battle got under way. From this main salient the line bent backward to the northwest, crossing the Hillsboro pike (Twenty-first Avenue South) just north of Blair Boulevard. Continuing a little north of west, the Federal line crossed the Natchez Trace at about its present intersection with Essex Avenue and extended to the top of the hill west of the Natchez Trace, reached now by Hillside and

Acting Rear Admiral S. Philips Lee, in charge of the Mississippi Squadron of inland war vessels, was the over-all chief of naval operations in this sector. Lieutenant Commander LeRoy Fitch commanded the squadron at Nashville and in its immediate vicinity, and he assumed the responsibility for patrolling the river above and below the city to guard against any unobserved crossing of the Cumberland by the Confederates.

Thomas got off to a bad start with the rank-conscious Admiral Lee. His telegram to Lee on November 30, asking that ironclads be assigned to the job of patrolling the Cumberland and convoying the transports that were bringing men and supplies to Nashville, was considered by Lee to be phrased in words which made it "an order instead of a request," and the admiral minced no words in rebuking the general for the impropriety of his mode of address. Thomas, however, had no inclination to make a serious issue of the matter. He apologized and thanked the admiral for his co-operation, and their relations were afterwards cordial and pleasant.[4]

Schofield and his force arrived in Nashville from

Overlook drives. From the crest of this hill the line turned northward and extended to the top of the hill now known as Love Circle, where an auxiliary reservoir is located; on top of this hill was an important work. From Love Circle the line ran across the Harding pike, along the high ground northeast of Minnesota Avenue, with a strong point on the hill west of Centennial Park, and ended on the railroad about where the spur track to West Nashville branches off. At this point the line was offset, but it picked up on the north side of the railroad a little further to the east—almost back to the present location of Centennial Park. There was a strong fortification on the high hill overlooking the Charlotte pike, the top of which is about at the corner of Thirty-third Avenue and Elkins Avenue. The next salient in the line was a hill just across the Charlotte pike on the north side; and thence the line continued along the row of knobs until it ended on the knoll on Centennial Boulevard overlooking the river, about where the Tennessee Agricultural and Industrial State University is now located.

4 *Official Records*, Vol. XLV, Pt. I, 1167; Pt. II, 18-19, 30.

Franklin during the forenoon of December 1, and by noon of that day Thomas had established his outer line of battle on the hills in front of and surrounding the city. Schofield's Twenty-third Corps was placed on the left, extending to the Nolensville pike. The Fourth Corps, now commanded by General Thomas J. Wood, following the wounding of General Stanley at Franklin, occupied the center. General Smith's divisions, as they arrived, were placed on the right of the line. Wilson and his cavalry at first occupied the interval between Schofield's left and the river above the city; but on December 3, when the cavalry moved to Edgefield on the north side of the river, the space left vacant by their withdrawal was occupied by the provisional division and other force commanded by Major General James B. Steedman.

Leaving a sufficient force at Franklin to bury the dead and care for the wounded, Hood started in pursuit of Schofield the morning of December 1, but even Forrest's cavalrymen were unable to overtake the fast-fleeing Federals, who were safe within the Nashville fortifications that afternoon. On the morning of December 2 Hood deployed on the hills south of Nashville what was left of the badly battered Army of Tennessee. The tragic events of the preceding few days at Spring Hill and Franklin not only had decimated the army's ranks but had seriously undermined its morale. A particularly demoralizing factor contributing heavily to the army's confusion and its lessened efficiency as a formidable fighting force was the extraordinarily heavy loss in commissioned officers at Franklin. The official report of casualties includes a total of sixty-six officers of the rank of captain and above.[5]

Those killed outright were Major General Patrick

5 *Ibid.*, Pt. I, 684-86.

Ronayne Cleburne and four brigadier generals: John Adams, Hiram Bronson Granbury, States Rights Gist and Otho French Strahl. Brigadier General George W. Gordon was captured at the time his brigade broke through the Federal lines in the first impetuous, momentarily successful assault. Major General John Calvin Brown was wounded, as were Brigadier Generals Arthur Middleton Manigault, Francis Marion Cockrell, William Andrew Quarles, Thomas Moore Scott and John Carpenter Carter, the latter fatally. In addition to these twelve general officers, six colonels, two lieutenant colonels, three majors and two captains were killed; fifteen colonels, nine lieutenant colonels, six majors and three captains were wounded; and two colonels, two majors and four captains were reported missing. Adding the final touch to the confusion in command, Major General Samuel Gibbs French was granted sick leave and on the very morning of the opening of the battle of Nashville, December 15, left his division as the opening guns sounded.

As a result of the unparalleled slaughter of officers at Franklin, there was hardly a brigade, regiment, or company in the army confronting Nashville that was not commanded by new and frequently strange and inexperienced officers, with a corresponding lack of understanding, confidence in leadership, and *esprit de corps*. In Cleburne's division the highest ranking officer left in Granbury's brigade was a captain, and many brigades were commanded by colonels, lieutenant colonels, and majors.

Hood himself, naturally enough, was depressed and chagrined. Depression and chagrin gave birth to desperation, and it was apparently this desperation, coupled with his natural and uncontrollable combativeness, that decided him at this time to challenge Thomas to battle. Hood was thoroughly aware of the disparity in numbers between his army and the Federal force defending Nashville. He should also have realized that the vague prospect of reinforcements from the Trans-Mississippi Department of the Confederacy was a vain hope.

Beauregard was in Montgomery when he got the sad news of the disastrous battle of Franklin, and he realized that something should be done at once to replace the men lost there if Hood's campaign was to be sustained. The Confederacy had been bled white of its recruitable material, and most of the armies in the field were so hard-pressed that there was now no possibility of borrowing temporarily from one to bolster up another. Longstreet could not now be shuttled out to the west to fight a battle and then shuttled back to Virginia, as had been done in 1863. At his wits' end for some source of additional manpower, Beauregard again turned to General Edmund Kirby Smith, out in the Trans-Mississippi Department. To him Beauregard sent a moving letter asking for assistance for Hood. "The fate of the country may depend upon the result of Hood's campaign in Tennessee," he wrote, asking Kirby Smith either to send "two or more divisions" to Hood or else to launch an offensive against Missouri which would prevent assistance being sent from there to Thomas.[6]

There was no mail service to the Trans-Mississippi and no telegraph line, so the letter was sent by one of Beauregard's staff officers, a copy of it being sent to President Davis, with a request for his influence with Kirby Smith. Secretary Seddon gave his official sanction to Beauregard's effort, but pessimistically expressed doubts as to Kirby Smith's willingness to help, glumly

6 *Ibid.*, Pt. II, 639.

remarking that "no plans should be based on his compliance."[7] Beauregard wrote to Kirby Smith again on December 13, and Seddon backed up this appeal with a direct personal message. But Secretary Seddon's misgivings were well founded. Kirby Smith at long last wrote a lengthy letter to Beauregard explaining in detail why he could do nothing to help Hood—but this was not until January 6, when Hood was beyond help.[8]

As the Confederates reached the outskirts of Nashville on their advance from Franklin, General Hood established his headquarters at Travelers' Rest, the home of John Overton on the Franklin pike six miles from Nashville, and immediately issued to his corps commanders an order covering the establishment of the Confederate line:

"General Lee will form his corps with his center upon the Franklin pike; General Stewart will form on General Lee's left; and General Cheatham on General Lee's right.

"The entire line of the army will curve forward from General Lee's center so that General Cheatham's right may come as near the Cumberland as possible above Nashville, and General Stewart's left as near the Cumberland as possible below Nashville. Each position will be strengthened as soon as taken, and extended as fast as strengthened. Artillery will be placed in all favorable positions. All engineer officers will be constantly engaged in examining the position of the enemy and looking to all his weak points. Corps commanders will give all necessary assistance. Not a cartridge of any kind will be burned until further orders, unless the enemy should advance on us."[9]

It immediately became apparent that there were not nearly enough of Hood's infantry to form a line which

[7] *Ibid.*, 647.   [8] *Ibid.*, 766.   [9] *Ibid.*, 640-41.

would come close to enveloping the Federal defensive fortifications from river to river. Cheatham's corps could reach no further to the right than just across the Nolensville pike, a mile from the river. Stewart, on the left, barely reached the Hillsboro pike, leaving an interval of four miles to the river.[10]

[10] General Hood's entrenched line at the time of the battle was hastily constructed, under adverse weather conditions. It was about four miles long, much shorter than the Federal lines of defense. The Confederate right wing rested at a deep cut on the Nashville and Chattanooga Railroad between the Nolensville and Murfreesboro pikes, about where that road now crosses the Lewisburg and Northern Railroad. Slightly in advance of the main line at this point, in the rear of the Rains (later Robinson) house, later called "Woodycrest," was a small lunette occupied by the 300 survivors of the brigade of General Granbury, who had been killed at Franklin. The main Confederate line crossed to the west of the Nolensville pike at about the present Peachtree Street, to the principal stronghold of the right flank on top of Rains's (or Riddle's) Hill, a commanding elevation. This flank was also protected by a line of two detached batteries, with a handful of infantry, extended southeastward, parallel to the pike, between the road and the railroad, giving to the right flank an unusual Y-shaped formation. Further to the right, south of the present Thompson Lane, a redoubt was later built on a high hill commanding the Murfreesboro pike and protecting the right of the Confederate position.

Extending to the west, Hood's line ran through the grounds of Melrose, the old home of Aaron V. Brown; then, continuing westward, it crossed the Franklin pike at about its intersection with Thompson's Lane, where a monument has been erected commemorating the battle. Thence the line ranged eastward across the farm where the late James E. Caldwell lived, just north of his residence and back of Brown's Creek, crossing the Granny White pike at a sharp angle with the road a short distance south of the present Woodmont Avenue. The line then ran along slightly south of the present location of Woodmont Avenue, crossing Woodmont at an acute angle, where the earthworks are still to be seen in front of the residence of Oscar W. Carter on the south side of the road and of Alfred Ehrenwald on the north side. Going on up the hill westward, the line reached Hood's main salient in a redoubt, known as Redoubt No. 1, which crowned the elevation north of Woodmont Avenue and east of the Hillsboro pike, in the rear of and southeast of the home of A. W. Brooks on Hillsboro. Here Hood's line turned sharply back southward at almost a right angle, crossing Woodmont still east of the Hillsboro pike to another fortified work, Redoubt No. 2, which stood just south of Woodmont and east of

To cover the excessive intervals between the infantry line and the Cumberland on both wings, Hood planned to use his cavalry. But the cavalry force also was inadequate to its assigned task—especially as Hood immediately dispersed Forrest's forces in a masterpiece of suicidal folly.

When the army was leaving Franklin on the morning of December 2, Cheatham was ordered by Hood to send his division commanded by Major General William Brimage Bate to Murfreesboro, about twenty-eight miles eastward, "to destroy the railroad from Murfrees-

---

Hillsboro, in the rear of the homes of P. C. Childs on Woodmont and Dr. Horace C. Gayden on Hillsboro. From Redoubt No. 2 the entrenched line extended diagonally across the pike to Redoubt No. 3, west of the Hillsboro pike, present location of Calvary Methodist Church and immediately adjoining the flower garden in the rear of the residence of J. T. Griscom, facing on the street now known as Hood's Hill Road. Further support for Hood's left was supplied by two more detached works west of the Hillsboro pike—Redoubt No. 4, located on the hill where Hobbs Road now is intersected by Trimble Road, about a half mile west of the pike; and Redoubt No. 5, on top of the high hill immediately to the west of the pike further out, where the residence of Dr. Stanley R. Teachout now stands. Work on Redoubts No. 4 and No. 5 had been delayed by the bad weather and the rocky nature of the ground, and they were scarcely finished on December 15, when the battle started.

Hood's engineers originally located his main line in a position which extended westward from Rains's Hill, crossing the Franklin pike about midway between the present Tennessee Central Railroad and Thompson Lane, crossing the Granny White pike at the intersection of Gale Lane, continuing to the top of the hill west of Belmont Boulevard reached by Cedar Lane. This hill was formerly the site of the Montgomery mansion, which had been burned, and it was known as Montgomery Hill. This line then extended along the brow of this elevation, facing the Federal main salient only a few hundred yards to the north, about as Cedar Lane now runs but slightly to the north of it, almost to the Hillsboro pike, where it turned back a short distance along the pike. It was later decided by Hood that this line was too close to the Federal position and was untenable, and the engineers located the stronger line to the rear; on December 10, this was occupied as the main line. The abandoned entrenchment was then lightly occupied as a skirmish line.

borough to Nashville, burning all the bridges and taking the block-houses and then burning them."[11] Bate's division consisted of three brigades of infantry: Tyler's, now commanded by Brigadier General Thomas Benton Smith; Finley's, commanded by Colonel Robert Bullock; and Brigadier General Henry Rootes Jackson's brigade. Including a battery of artillery, Bate's total force was about 1,600 men. When Bate approached Murfreesboro, he discovered that the town, instead of having been evacuated as Hood had supposed, was held by a force of from 6,000 to 10,000 men under Major General Rousseau, which fact he reported to Hood on the morning of December 4. Hood replied that "Forrest will send some of his cavalry to assist you," but reminded Bate that the object of his expedition was "to destroy the railroad."[12]

The Confederate cavalry under Forrest had pursued Schofield's retreating army from Franklin on December 1, but they were not able to do anything more than harass its rear guard. Forrest's men bivouacked that night on a line stretching from the Nolensville to the Granny White pike, in sight of the Capitol building at Nashville. The next day Hood divided Forrest's force, assigning the division of Major General James Ronald Chalmers to duty on the left of the Confederate line, between Stewart's left and the river. Forrest's other two divisions, under Major Generals Abraham Buford and William Hicks Jackson, were stationed on the Confederate right. They created considerable alarm in Nashville by immediately engaging in some spirited skirmishing with the outposts on the Federal left, and a large crowd assembled on the Capitol Hill to watch the flashes of the guns and listen to the roar, as the forts opened their heavy artillery fire on the Confederates. All this, however, was only a little unimportant byplay as far as Forrest was concerned, as he had been ordered to put these two divisions to work on the Nashville and Chattanooga Railroad, proceeding in the direction of Murfreesboro, destroying the railroad bridges and the guarding blockhouses as they went along.

By December 5 Forrest and his railroad-wrecking troopers had worked their way south of Lavergne, leaving a ruined railroad in their wake. Then, under orders from Hood, Forrest joined forces with Bate and assumed command of the combined body of cavalry and infantry. Further augmenting Forrest's command were two small infantry brigades under Sears and Palmer which joined him that evening, giving him a total force of something less than 6,000 men, with which he was ordered to assume offensive operations against Murfreesboro. Forrest recognized the futility of attacking Rousseau's much larger force in the Murfreesboro breastworks but hoped to entice a portion of the Federal garrison out of the fortifications and attack them in the open country outside the town. Rousseau obliged by sending out about half his force under General Milroy, Stonewall Jackson's early victim in Virginia, and Forrest fell on Milroy along Overall's Creek, south of the site of the earlier big-scale battle between Bragg and Rosecrans. Milroy was driven back into the town, but the engagement could hardly be considered a Confederate success. Forrest reported that the infantry, with the exception of Benton Smith's brigade, acted badly and made "a shameful retreat"; Bate reported that the cavalry gave ground "with but slight resistance."

At any rate, Bate's division was recalled to Nashville on December 9 and took its place in Cheatham's line there, being replaced at Murfreesboro by General James

A. Smith's old brigade, now under Colonel Charles H. Olmstead. Buford's division of cavalry was sent back to the neighborhood of the Hermitage, east of Nashville, assigned to the duty of watching the Cumberland River and in general protecting that flank. Forrest, with Jackson's division, continued his assignment aimed at the destructon of the railroad around Murfreesboro. In the course of this operation they had the pleasure of capturing and burning a supply train of seventeen cars which was coming into Murfreesboro from the south, and of taking 200 prisoners—but Forrest was far removed from the scene of the impending battle, and his absence would be sorely felt.

General Chalmers meanwhile was doing his best to take care of the rather large assignment that had been handed him—covering the four-mile interval between the left of Stewart's infantry line on the Hillsboro pike and the Cumberland River. To perform this duty he had only his one division of cavalry, comprised of the two brigades commanded by Colonel Edmund W. Rucker and Colonel Jacob B. Biffle. Establishing his headquarters at the Belle Meade mansion, home of General W. G. Harding on the Harding pike, he disposed his force to the best possible advantage. A regiment (300 men) under Lieutenant Colonel David C. Kelley was sent with two pieces of artillery to a point on the river bluff opposite Bell's Mill, twelve miles below Nashville, effectually blockading the river, although Kelley got in position just a day too late to interfere with the transports bringing A. J. Smith's Corps to Nashville. The remainder of Chalmers' mounted force was strung out, protecting the Harding and Charlotte pikes.

On December 10 Chalmers was ordered to send Biffle's brigade to the right wing of the Confederate line to support Buford in that quarter, leaving Rucker's brigade the only cavalry force on the Confederate left. "I wrote to General Hood," Chalmers says in his official report of the battle, "showing the strength of my command and the length of the line which I was expected to hold, and that it would be imposible for me to maintain my position if attacked unless supported. On the 14th Ector's brigade of infantry was sent to relieve my force on the Hardin pike, and my line then extended from the left of that pike across the Charlotte pike to the river, a distance of about four miles, to defend which and to support the batteries on the river I had a force of 900 aggregate present, the Seventh Alabama Cavalry being between Ector's brigade and the left of the main line of infantry."[13]

General Matthew D. Ector had lost a leg at Atlanta, and his brigade was now commanded by Colonel David Coleman of the Thirty-ninth North Carolina. The brigade had suffered severely at Franklin, being now reduced to 700 men, and it made but a thin line. The principal part of this force was placed in hastily prepared breastworks behind Richland Creek, north of the Harding pike, on the high ground west of the present buildings of the Veterans' Administration. A skirmish line was thrown out on the other side of the creek, closer to Nashville, and a picket line was placed across the Harding pike.

The Seventh Alabama Cavalry on Ector's right was doing its best to cover the wide interval between the Harding and Hillsboro pikes. On Ector's left Rucker's cavalry brigade was covering the Charlotte pike, in position "back of the Cockrill place and north of the pike," about where the industrial center of West Nashville is now located. Two additional Parrott guns had been

[13] *Ibid.*, 764-65.

sent to Colonel Kelley on the river bluff, and he was banging away at any of the Federal craft that ventured within range of his guns.

So, as the zero hour approached, Forrest's mounted men were divided into individually impotent units, so disposed that the full burden of meeting the opening onslaught of the attacking Federals would fall on one lone brigade, supported by one depleted brigade of foot soldiers.

Hood made numerous errors of judgment in carrying out his plans, but none more suicidal than this. He knew, or should have known, that Thomas was building up a well-equipped cavalry force of greatly superior numbers, and that it would take all the strength he could muster to meet this force when it was ready to move. He knew that he had in Forrest a cavalry leader of the very highest ability who, even with lesser numbers, could be depended on to stand up effectively against the numerically superior Federal cavalry in the battle about to be fought. To dissipate the energies of Forrest and his command at this critical moment was a military blunder of colossal proportions. Within the next forty-eight hours it was to be demonstrated that the Federal cavalry was the deciding factor in the battle, as it provided the mobility, driving power, and punch that on two successive days turned the Confederate flank and crumbled Hood's defensive line. If this cavalry turning movement had been faced by Forrest himself, with his full concentrated force, instead of meeting only one of his brigades, there might have been a different story to tell.

Even General Wilson himself admitted that the absence of Forrest and the bulk of his cavalry made the Federals' task easier when the battle was fought. Wilson points out that every infantry attack on Hood's center and right, on both days of the battle, had been at first repulsed and makes the reasonable claim that had the cavalry's turning movement failed, Thomas' general plan would have been defeated. Although Wilson is reluctant to admit that had Forrest been present with all his force on Hood's left flank he would have been able to hold it, he does concede that "he could have made a better and more stubborn defense than was made by Chalmers and Ector alone"[14]—which is fairly obvious.

14 Wilson, *Under the Old Flag*, II, 120.

III

Preparations for Battle

THE treacherous December weather continued fair and mild from the second through the eighth, and the Confederates spent the week feverishly throwing up their breastworks along the high ground selected by the engineers, fronting the Federal position. But on the night of December 8 there came a sudden change. A cold rain mixed with snow began to fall, the temperature dropped rapidly, and the next morning the frozen ground was covered with snow and sleet. Then for a week there was rain, freezing rain and more sleet. The whole country around Nashville was covered with a sheet of ice. The movement of troops was extremely difficult, and the digging of trenches, practically impossible.

This abrupt and unseasonable change in the weather was a tremendous handicap to the Confederates. Not only did it put a stop to their vitally important work of entrenchment, but it was a source of the most intense suffering to the shivering, poorly clad men in the ranks. Hood was far from a source of supplies, with an attenuated line of communication. There was a sad lack of shoes, clothing, hats, and blankets. Occasional trains from Decatur brought in food supplies and some dribbles of jackets, breeches, and even underwear, but shoes were a virtually unknown luxury and so were hats and caps. A large proportion of the men were barefooted and many were bareheaded. Such tents as they had once possessed were now mostly left far behind, but those of them who had blankets or oilcloths used them to improvise shelter which they shared with their less fortunate fellows. When beeves were butchered the raw hides were issued, as far as they would go, to those most in need. Where cobblers could be found in the ranks, it was possible to procure some makeshift kind of shoes; otherwise, the soldiers wrapped the pieces of hide around their raw and bleeding feet and were thankful for even that protection. But only a fortunate few were able to get even such crude footwear, and thousands of Hood's men remained barefooted as the sleet and snow pelted down on their bare heads and froze their threadbare, ragged clothing.

The inclement weather did not cause such acute physical suffering among the well-fed, well-clothed, and comfortably quartered Federals, but it put a stop to Thomas' plans for battle and was the indirect cause of great disturbance among the high command of the army. Ever since Hood's arrival in front of Nashville, the authorities in Washington had been frantically nagging Thomas to move out and assault him without delay. General Grant, at his headquarters before Petersburg, was a long way from the scene of action and correspondingly ignorant of the conditions prevailing there, but he was so seriously impressed with the grave military and political potentialities of Hood's advance into Tennessee that he completely lost his customary calm and poise. Goaded by President Lincoln and Secretary Stanton, he became almost hysterical in his urging of Thomas to move immediately in aggressive action against the Confederates, regardless of his unpreparedness for such action.

Immediately following the battle of Franklin, Thomas had reported to General Halleck that he planned to remain on the defensive in the Nashville fortifications until General Wilson could get his cavalry equipped. This was duly reported to Lincoln, and on December 2 Stanton telegraphed Grant: "The President feels solicitous about the disposition of General Thomas to lay in fortifications for an indefinite period 'until Wilson gets equipments.' This looks like the Mc-Clellan and Rosecrans strategy of do nothing and let the rebels raid the country. The President wishes you to consider the matter."[1]

Thus nudged by the armchair strategists in Washington, Grant immediately telegraphed Thomas: "If Hood is permitted to remain quietly about Nashville, you will lose all the road back to Chattanooga, and possibly have to abandon the line of the Tennessee. Should he attack you it is all well, but if he does not you should attack him before he fortifies." Then, less than three hours later the same day, Grant prodded him again: "With your citizen employés armed, you can move out of Nashville with all your army and force the enemy to retire or fight upon ground of your own choosing. After the repulse of Hood at Franklin, it looks to me that instead of falling back to Nashville, we should have taken the offensive against the enemy where he was. . . . You will now suffer incalculable injury upon your railroads, if Hood is not speedily disposed of. Put forth, therefore, every possible exertion to attain this end."[2]

Nettled though he must have been by this long-distance needling by uninformed superiors, Thomas replied promptly that night: "At the time that Hood was whipped at Franklin, I had at this place but about 5,000 men of General Smith's command, which added to the force under General Schofield would not have given me more than 25,000 men; besides, General Schofield felt convinced that he could not hold the enemy at Franklin

[1] *Official Records*, Vol. XLV, Pt. II, 3, 15-16.   [2] *Ibid.*, 17.

until the 5,000 could reach him." He explained that the remainder of Smith's reinforcements had arrived just the preceding day, as well as the force of about 5,000 under General Steedman which had been ordered up from Chattanooga. "I now have infantry enough to assume the offensive, if I had more cavalry," he said, "and will take the field anyhow as soon as the remainder of General McCook's division of cavalry reaches here, which I hope it will do in two or three days." In a later telegram the same day, to Halleck, he again mentioned the necessity for reorganizing, remounting, and equipping "a cavalry force sufficient to contend with Forrest," and also stated that "The iron-clads and gun-boats are so disposed as to prevent Hood from crossing the river."[3]

The acute need for reorganizing, remounting, and equipping the cavalry was very real. Since the contending forces had crossed Duck River on November 29, Wilson's troopers had been roughly handled by Forrest's seasoned riders, and they showed the effects of it. Croxton on December 2 reported that his command was "shattered by long and severe service, . . . needs rest, and must have it." General Hammond reported on the same day that the men of his brigade were "tired and sluggish."[4] Thomas, as an experienced old cavalry officer, was well aware of the vital necessity for maintaining the efficiency of this branch of the service. Accordingly, on December 2 he ordered Wilson to move his cavalry corps to Edgefield on the north bank of the Cumberland across from Nashville and get to work shoeing the horses, putting in requisitions for clothing, and employing "all means necessary" to render the command efficient.[5]

3 *Ibid.*, 17-18.   4 *Ibid.*, 24, 26.   5 *Ibid.*, 24.

Thomas, meanwhile, was bending every energy to accumulate a sufficient supply of horses to remount the unmounted cavalrymen who had been ordered to report to him. Every horse in Nashville and its environs was impressed—carriage horses, work horses, plow horses, even the performing horses of a stray circus that happened to be in town at the time. Horses were being sent to Nashville from Louisville and elsewhere. The quartermaster was also moving heaven and earth to relieve the acute shortage of "long forage" (the then-current Army jargon for hay) which had resulted from Forrest's destruction of the supply depot at Johnsonville a few weeks previously.

The evening of December 3 Thomas telegraphed Halleck, reported that he had a good entrenched line around Nashville, and hoped to be able to have 10,000 cavalry mounted and equipped "in less than a week," and that he would then march against Hood. Meanwhile he was not taking any chances of a surprise attack by the Confederates, and on that same day orders were issued to all his division commanders to have reveille at 4:30 A.M. and the troops under arms by daylight every day, with division officers of the day and picket officers on the line instructed to report any movement of the Confederates.[6]

Although Grant was personally pretty well occupied with his own immediate problems incident to the seige of Lee at Petersburg, which was not progressing any too well, he seemed to spend much of his time worrying about affairs in Tennessee. On December 5 he telegraphed Thomas, expressing fear that Forrest might move down the Cumberland River and make a crossing. He said pointedly that while Thomas was getting

6 *Ibid.*, 29, 33.

his cavalry ready, "Hood should be attacked where he is," going on to say: "Time strengthens him, in all probability, as much as it does you."[7]

Thomas replied promptly: "If I can perfect my arrangements I shall move against the advanced position of the enemy on the 7th instant." But this did not satisfy Grant, who on the next day telegraphed Thomas peremptorily: "Attack Hood at once, and wait no longer for a remount of your cavalry. There is great danger of delay resulting in a campaign back to the Ohio River." Thomas had telegraphed Grant an hour before receiving this: "As soon as I can get up a respectable force of cavalry I will march against Hood.... I do not think it prudent to attack Hood with less than 6,000 cavalry to cover my flanks, because he has, under Forrest, at least 12,000." (Actually, Hood had less than 1,200 cavalry with him at this time.)

Upon receipt of the "Attack Hood at once" order, however, Thomas dutifully replied: "I will make the necessary dispositions and attack Hood at once, agreeably to your order, though I believe it will be hazardous with the small force of cavalry now at my service." As Thomas' biographer later wrote, however, in his effort to fulfill this promise "he met with obstacles that convinced him that he could not then fight a battle with such results as desired, and consequently he resolved, though with the consciousness of great personal hazard, to wait until the 9th or 10th."[8]

Stanton, upon reading Thomas' dispatch of December 6, telegraphed Grant at City Point: "Thomas seems unwilling to attack because it is hazardous, as if all war was anything but hazardous. If he waits for Wilson to get ready, Gabriel will be blowing his last horn." Thus goaded and supported by his superior's sneers, Grant

[7] *Ibid.,* 55.   [8] *Ibid.,* 55, 70; Van Horne, *Life of Thomas,* 303.

replied that he had ordered Thomas to attack and that "If he does not do it promptly, I would recommend superseding him by Schofield, leaving Thomas subordinate." The next day, December 8, he telegraphed Halleck: "If Thomas has not struck yet, he ought to be ordered to hand over the command to Schofield. There is no better man to repel an attack than Thomas, but I fear he is too cautious to ever take the initiative."[9]

Thereupon Halleck and Grant engaged in some cautious long-range verbal sparring. Halleck, having provoked Grant into action, seems to have weakened to the extent that he himself wished to have no part in Thomas' removal. He told Grant pointedly that if he wished Thomas relieved of his command he should himself give the order to have it done and that nobody in the War Department would interfere. "The responsibility, however, will be yours," Halleck told him bluntly, "as no one here, so far as I am informed, wishes General Thomas' removal." Grant then hedged: "I want General Thomas reminded of the importance of immediate action. I sent him a dispatch this evening which will probably urge him on. I would not say relieve him until I hear further from him."[10]

In this dispatch to Thomas, Grant had said: "It looks to me evident the enemy are trying to cross the Cumberland River and are scattered. Why not attack at once? By all means avoid the contingency of a foot race to see which, you or Hood, can beat to the Ohio." This advice must have mystified Thomas, who was on the ground and knew that the Confederates were not scattered and not trying to cross the river. Apparently, however, Grant had some private (and unreliable) source of information in Nashville, for on the morning of December 9 he telegraphed Halleck: "Dispatch of 8 p.m. last

[9] *Official Records*, Vol. XLV, Pt. II, 84, 96.   [10] *Ibid.*, 96.

evening from Nashville shows the enemy scattered for
more than seventy miles down the river, and no attack
yet made by Thomas. Please telegraph orders relieving
him at once and placing Schofield in command. Thomas
should be ordered to turn over all orders and dispatches
received since the battle of Franklin to Schofield."[11]

Presumably Grant did actually receive from some-
body some such dispatch as that quoted in his telegram
to Halleck, but there is no record of it anywhere in the
official archives. The *Official Records* do show that on
December 9 there was issued by the War Department
a document entitled "General Orders No. ____," which
read: "In accordance with the following dispatch from
Lieutenant-General Grant, viz—'Please telegraph order
relieving him (General Thomas) at once and placing
Schofield in command. Thomas should be directed to
turn over all dispatches received since the battle of
Franklin to Schofield. U. S. Grant, Lieutenant General.'
The President orders: I. That Maj. Gen. J. M. Schofield
assume command of all troops in the Departments of
the Cumberland, the Ohio and the Tennessee. II. That
Maj. Gen. George H. Thomas report to General Schofield for duty and turn over to him all orders and dispatches received by him, as specified. By order of the
Secretary of War: [blanks for signature]."[12]

So far as can be discovered, this unsigned and un-
numbered "General Orders" was never actually promulgated or officially communicated to the individuals
involved. On the morning of December 9, however,
Halleck telegraphed Thomas that Grant "expresses
much dissatisfaction at your delay in attacking the enemy. If you wait till General Wilson mounts all his

---

[11] *Ibid.*, 97, 115-16; Ephraim A. Otis, *The Nashville Campaign* (Chicago, 1899), 278.
[12] *Official Records*, Vol. XLV, Pt. II, 114.

cavalry, you will wait till doomsday." Thomas replied to Halleck, expressing regret at Grant's dissatisfaction and saying: "I feel conscious that I have done everything in my power to prepare, and that the troops could not have been gotten ready before this, and if he should order me to be relieved I will submit without a murmur. A terrible storm of freezing rain has come on since daylight, which will render an attack impossible until it breaks."

He also telegraphed Grant the same day, replying to Grant's dispatch of the preceding evening: "I had nearly completed my preparations to attack the enemy to-morrow morning, but a terrible storm of freezing rain has come on to-day, which will make it impossible for our men to fight to any advantage. I am, therefore, compelled to wait for the storm to break and make the attack immediately after." Thomas' knowledge of the conditions immediately confronting him made it obvious to him that no effective attack could be made in the existing circumstances. His soldierly conscience, however, was disturbed by his knowledge of the fact that he was deliberately disobeying his superior's orders, so he respectfully closed his message with the words: "Major-General Halleck informs me that you are very much dissatisfied with my delay in attacking. I can only say I have done all in my power to prepare, and if you should deem it necessary to relieve me I shall submit without a murmur." [13]

As a matter of fact, although Thomas did not deign to defend himself by going into details, at the very time these telegrams were burning the wires between Nashville, Washington, and City Point, he had already issued formal, detailed orders to his corps commanders for an attack on the Confederate positions to be launched at

[13] *Ibid.*, 114, 115.

daylight on December 10. When the abrupt change in the weather made this movement physically impracticable, the corps leaders were notified on the ninth that "it is found necessary to postpone the operations designed for to-morrow morning until the breaking up of the storm." Thomas instructed, however, that everything be put in condition to carry out the attack as soon as the weather would permit, "so that we can act instantly when the storm clears away."[14]

Upon receipt of Thomas' message of December 9 Halleck decided to hold up the dispatch relieving Thomas of his command and so notified Grant, stating, "If you still wish these orders telegraphed to Nashville they will be forwarded." Grant replied that evening that "I am very unwilling to do injustice to an officer who has done as much good service as General Thomas has, . . . and will, therefore, suspend the order relieving him until it is seen whether he will do anything." To Thomas he sent a grudging and ungracious message: "Your dispatch of 1 p.m. received. I have as much confidence in your conducting a battle rightly as I have in any other officer; but it has seemed to me that you have been slow, and I have had no explanation of affairs to convince me otherwise. Receiving your dispatch of 2 p.m. from General Halleck, before I did the one to me, I telegraphed to suspend the order relieving you until we should hear further. I hope most sincerely that there will be no necessity of repeating the orders, and that the facts will show that you have been right all the time."[15]

Grant's reference to suspending "the order relieving you" seems to indicate that he understood that Thomas knew of such an order; and in his *Personal Memoirs* he states that after sending Thomas frequent orders to attack at once, "At last I had to say to General Thomas

14 *Ibid.,* 118.   15 *Ibid.,* 115, 116.

that I should be obliged to remove him unless he acted promptly."[16] Nowhere in the official records, however, is there any communication from Grant to Thomas intimating that Thomas was confronted with the alternative of attacking or losing his command. On the other hand, when in 1870 the loquacious General Halleck stated in a newspaper interview that Grant had asked for Thomas' removal in favor of Schofield just before the battle, it is recorded that Thomas read this with surprise. "That he had come close to being displaced," one of his biographers writes, "was something which Thomas had never known but had always suspected."[17]

That Thomas had ample room for suspicion is indicated by the story this biographer tells of what was going on in Nashville in those tense days just before the battle: "General Whipple, Thomas's chief of staff, began to declare that someone was using the wires to undermine his commander at Washington. Thomas sent for Steedman, able veteran of Chickamauga. Could it be Governor Johnson? he asked. Steedman did not think so. He had talked with Johnson and knew him to be above-board at least. Thomas suggested that he look into the matter. Steedman returned to his headquarters and assigned some detective work to an aide. This officer, Captain Marshall Davis, went to the telegraph office and picked up a message from Schofield to Grant: 'Many officers here are of the opinion that General Thomas is certainly too slow in his movements.' Steedman hastened with the message to Thomas, who examined it carefully and inquired, 'Steedman, can it be possible that Schofield would send such a telegram?' Steedman remarked that Thomas should be familiar with the

16 *Personal Memoirs of U. S. Grant,* 567.
17 Freeman Cleaves, *Rock of Chickamauga* (Norman, Okla., 1948), 304.

handwriting of his own general. Thomas put on his glasses and held up the message before the light. 'Yes, it is General Schofield's handwriting. . . . Why does he send such telegrams?' Several years later Steedman recalled that he 'smiled at the noble old soldier's simplicity and said: "General Thomas, who is next in command to you and would succeed you in case of removal?" "Oh, I see," he said as he mournfully shook his head.' "[18]

General Steedman reiterated these charges in an article which appeared in the New York *Times*, June 22, 1881, making the blunt assertion that "General Thomas knew three days before the battle of Nashville that Schofield was playing the part of Judas by telegraphing to General Grant disparaging suggestions about the action of Thomas," and that "it was known to a number of our officers that Schofield was intriguing with Grant to get Thomas relieved, in order that he might succeed to the command of our army." This provoked a denial and countercharges from Schofield, but it was hard to believe that Steedman had invented his story out of thin air.

At any rate, on the evening of that icy December 10 in Nashville, Thomas invited his corps commanders to meet with him in his room at the St. Cloud Hotel in an informal conference. Here, in the words of his biographer, Van Horne, "he made known to them the nature of the orders he had received from General Grant and that he had decided that obedience was impracticable," and the other generals "unanimously sustained General Thomas in his purpose to withhold battle until the ice should melt."[19]

It will be observed that no mention is made of Thomas' stating that he had been threatened with the

[18] *Ibid.*, 259.   [19] Van Horne, *Life of Thomas*, 320.

loss of his command, and General Wilson, who later wrote an account of the conference, does not refer to any such startling revelation by the army commander. But Schofield, in his memoirs, relates that when Thomas called his corps commanders to this conference he informed them that he was ordered "to attack Hood at once or surrender his command (not saying to whom), and asked our advice as to what he ought to do."

Schofield goes on to say: "One of the officers present asked Thomas to show us the order, which he declined to do. This confirmed the belief which I had at first formed that the successor named by General Grant could be no other than myself—a belief formed from the fact that I was, next to General Thomas, the highest officer in rank on the ground where immediate action was demanded, and from my knowledge of General Grant's confidence, which belief has since been fully justified by the record. This, as I conceived, imposed upon me the duty of responding at once to General Thomas's request for advice, without waiting for the junior members of the council, according to the usual military custom. Hence I immediately replied: 'General Thomas, I will sustain you in your determination not to fight until you are fully ready.' All the other commanders then promptly expressed their concurrence."[20]

Wilson, in his account of the conference, not only does not say that Thomas told them that he must surrender his command if he did not attack but tells a story which otherwise varies materially from Schofield's. He relates that as he was the junior corps commander present, in years as well as in rank, he spoke first and expressed his full approval of the course Thomas had adopted. In his youthful exuberance Wilson declared that under the existing conditions, the ground covered

[20] Schofield, *Forty-six Years in the Army*, 238.

with ice, "if I were occupying such an intrenched line as Hood's with my dismounted cavalrymen, each armed with nothing more formidable than a basket of brickbats, I would agree to defeat the whole Confederate army if it should advance to the attack under such circumstances." Wilson states that Smith, Wood, and Steedman were equally outspoken in their endorsement of Thomas' postponement of action. "But," he goes on, "Schofield . . . sat silent, and by that means alone, if at all, concurred in the judgment of those present that Thomas's course first and last was fully justified by the circumstances and conditions which confronted him. It was doubtless this silence that gave rise to the suspicion on the part of Steedman, and possibly of Thomas himself, that Schofield was already in touch with Grant or the War Department."

Wilson relates further that when the others withdrew Thomas asked him to remain for further conference, and said to him: "Wilson, the Washington authorities treat me as if I was a boy. . . . If they will just let me alone I will show them what we can do. I am sure my plan of operations is correct, and that we shall lick the enemy if he only stays to receive our attack."[21]

Thomas' outburst to Wilson reveals the fact that, for all the dignity of his official position, he was still just a human being and felt "bitterness and resentment" (to use Wilson's words) at being censured and lectured by Grant. Grant, as Thomas did not hesitate to remind Wilson, was having troubles of his own in Virginia, where he had a force of 100,000 veterans confronting Lee's numerically inferior force but had himself been able to do nothing more than settle down "in a listless deadlock." Grant, it seemed to Thomas, was in no position to censure any other general for inactivity.

21 Wilson, *Under the Old Flag*, II, 100-102.

Grant, for his part, certainly did not entertain any very friendly feeling for Thomas. His animosity was based on the resentment he had felt when Thomas was advanced after the capture of Corinth and Grant was shorn of authority until he was, as he bitterly expressed it, "a mere observer." Schofield, too, was nursing a grudge against Thomas, which went back to the time when he was a student at West Point and for some misconduct was court-martialed and sentenced to be dismissed. Thomas was a member of the court, and he declined to recommend that the sentence be remitted. A majority of the court did vote to restore Schofield to the service and his military career continued; but he never forgave Thomas for "this stern denial of clemency to a youth."[22]

Thus long-nursed grudges, wounded feelings, and personal resentments played like flickering sheet lightning in the background, as the battle clouds gathered lower about Nashville.

The morning following his reassuring conference with his corps commanders on the evening of December 10, Thomas received another telegram from the jittery Grant: "If you delay attack longer the mortifying spectacle will be witnessed of a rebel army moving for the Ohio River, and you will be forced to act, accepting such weather as you find. Let there be no further delay. Hood cannot stand even a drawn battle, so far from his supplies of ordinance stores. . . . Delay no longer for weather or re-enforcements."

Thomas, of course, had not intimated that he was delaying for reinforcements, but he waived this point and respectively replied: "I will obey the order as promptly as possible, however much I may regret it, as the attack will have to be made under every disadvantage. The

22 *Ibid.*, 105; Schofield, *Forty-six Years in the Army*, 242.

whole country is covered with a perfect sheet of ice and sleet, and it is with difficulty the troops are able to move about on level ground. It was my intention to attack Hood as soon as the ice melted, and would have done so yesterday had it not been for the storm." And to Halleck he sent a dispatch stating: "The weather continues very cold and the hills are covered with ice. As soon as we have a thaw, I will attack Hood."[23]

Before hearing from Grant on December 11, Thomas had begun to make the final preparations necessary for launching his attack. Orders were issued to his infantry corps commanders, Schofield, Smith, Wood and Steedman: "Have your command put in readiness to-morrow for operations. I wish to see you at my headquarters at 3 p.m. tomorrow." On the same day he ordered General Wilson to "commence the crossing of your command over the river to-morrow morning, as positive orders have been received to at once attack the enemy. They will go into position as has already been designated."[24]

As the infantry commanders proceeded with their preparations, Wilson issued orders to his four division leaders, Generals Edward Hatch, Richard W. Johnson, John T. Croxton and Joseph F. Knipe, to cross the river from Edgefield to Nashville early the next morning, Hatch and Johnson by way of the pontoon bridge which had been constructed near the foot of Church Street, and Croxton and Knipe on the planked-over railroad bridge. They moved to the western outskirts of the city and took position in the rear of Smith's infantry there, but not without great difficulty, as mentioned in Thomas' dispatch to Halleck on the evening of December 12: "I have the troops ready to make the attack on the enemy as soon as the sleet which now covers the

[23] *Official Records*, Vol. XLV, Pt. II, 143.   [24] *Ibid.*, 147, 148.

ground has melted sufficiently to enable the men to march. As the whole country is now covered with a sheet of ice so hard and slippery it is utterly impossible for troops to ascend the slopes, or even move over level ground in anything like order. It has taken the entire day to place my cavalry in position, and it has only been finally effected with imminent risk and many serious accidents, resulting from the number of horses falling with their riders on the road. Under these circumstances I believe an attack at this time would only result in a useless sacrifice of life."[25]

But everybody knew that the thaw could not be much longer delayed and that it was now only a matter of hours until the battle should begin. In preparation for the impending attack, orders were issued on the twelfth to all division commanders to have their men fully supplied with such clothing as they might need, and to see to it that each man had in his haversack three days' rations, as well as sixty rounds of ammunition. It was also ordered that all preparations be made for active operations—that the supply trains be loaded and ready to move, ammunition trains fully loaded, and artillery horses rough-shod.[26] There was a bustle of orderly confusion all along the line as the time grew closer and closer for the rising of the curtain.

With all possible preparations made, there was now nothing for Thomas to do but wait as patiently as he could for the weather to break. For two days the men stood ready to move, but winter's icy grip continued. Then, on the morning of December 14 there was a welcome rise in the temperature, and under a warm sun the ice and the frozen ground melted rapidly. Thomas immediately began putting the final touches

[25] *Ibid.*, 155.   [26] *Ibid.*, 156, 158.

on his long-deferred plans, preparatory to launching his attack on Hood the next morning; but in the midst of these activities he received another querulous telegram from Halleck: "It has been seriously apprehended that while Hood, with a part of his forces, held you in check near Nashville, he would have time to operate against other important points left only partially protected. Hence, General Grant was anxious that you should attack the rebel force in your front, and expressed great dissatisfaction that his orders had not been carried out. Moreover, so long as Hood occupies a threatening position in Tennessee, General Canby is obliged to keep large forces upon the Mississippi River, to protect its navigation and to hold Memphis, Vicksburg, &c., although General Grant had directed a part of these forces to co-operate with General Sherman. Every day's delay on your part, therefore, seriously interferes with General Grant's plans." Restraining what must have been a strong temptation to comment on the new and extraneous issue of General Edward R. S. Canby, Thomas simply filed a telegram in reply: "The ice having melted away to-day, the enemy will be attacked to-morrow morning. Much as I regret the apparent delay in attacking the enemy, it could not have been done before with any reasonable hope of success."[27]

Nothing was said about it in Halleck's dispatch, but on the previous day there had been a startling and important development—a development which, if Thomas had been informed of it, would probably have blasted even his imperturbable calm. The fuming Grant, his impatience finally conquering his judgment and whatever sense of military etiquette he may have had, had ordered Major General John A. Logan to proceed from

27 *Ibid.,* 180.

Washington to Nashville and take over the command from Thomas—provided Thomas had made no advance when Logan arrived. Then, still tortured by his doubts and his fears, Grant had come to the conclusion that the situation at Nashville was of such critically grave importance and so fraught with possibilities of great disaster that he had better give his personal attention; and so, on the heels of Logan, he started for Nashville himself.

Grant arrived in Washington on the afternoon of December 15 and upon inquiry found that telegraphic communication with Nashville had been interrupted by wire trouble and that no news had been received from Thomas for twenty-four hours. After conferring with Lincoln, Stanton, and Halleck, Grant told them that he intended to go on to Nashville and take command there in person, meanwhile relieving Thomas and putting Schofield in his place. An order removing Thomas was written by Grant and handed to Major Thomas T. Eckert, who was in charge of the War Department telegraph office, to be dispatched to Nashville. By this time the wire service had been restored, but Eckert was apparently sympathetic to Thomas and he took it upon himself to hold up the message until more news arrived from Nashville. Finally, at nearly midnight, the instruments in the War Office started clicking, and there came over the wires Thomas' delayed message to Halleck of the preceding evening, announcing his readiness to give battle the next morning. Then, close on the heels of this official dispatch, came a message to Eckert from the Nashville telegraph operator giving the news of the victory won by Thomas that day. Eckert took this message to Lincoln at the White House and to Stanton at his home, and they were duly elated at the news. Eckert admitted then to Stanton that he had not sent the message relieving Thomas, and Stanton, in his elation, absolved him of blame.[28]

Meanwhile, unaware of all this, Thomas was proceeding carefully and methodically with his plans for giving battle to Hood. At 3 P.M. on December 14 he called his corps commanders into a second council of war at his St. Cloud Hotel headquarters and discussed with them all the details of his plans for the operation he intended to launch the next morning. The plan of battle was the same as had been outlined in the orders issued for the attack that had been planned for the morning of the tenth, so all those present were familiar with what was intended. In recognition of the fact that the commanders of his infantry corps were from three distinct Federal army organizations, he deferentially asked for their views before announcing his plans. Then, after listening to all they had to say, he handed to each of them his Special Field Orders No. 342, outlining precisely what each of the bodies of troops were expected to do:

"First. Maj. Gen. A. J. Smith, commanding Detachment of the Army of the Tennessee, after forming his troops on and near the Hardin Pike, in front of his present position, will make a vigorous assault on the enemy's left.

"Second. Bvt. Maj. Gen. J. H. Wilson, commanding the Cavalry Corps, Military Division of the Mississippi, with three divisions, will move on and support General Smith's right, assist as far as possible in carrying the left of the enemy's position, and be in readiness to throw his force upon the enemy the moment a favorable opportunity occurs. Major-General Wilson will also send

28 David Homer Bates, *Lincoln in the Telegraph Office* (New York, 1939), 315 *et seq.*

one division on the Charlotte pike to clear that road of the enemy and observe in the direction of Bell's Landing, to protect our right rear until the enemy's position is fairly turned, when it will join the main force.

"Third. Brig. Gen. Th. J. Wood, commanding Fourth Army Corps, after leaving a strong skirmish line in his works from Laurens' [Lawrence] Hill to his extreme right, will form the remainder of the Fourth Corps on the Hillsborough pike to support General Smith's left and operate on the left and rear of the enemy's advanced position on the Montgomery Hill.

"Fourth. Maj. Gen. John M. Schofield, commanding Twenty-third Army Corps, will replace Brigadier-General Kimball's division, of the Fourth Corps, with his troops, and occupy the trenches from Fort Negley to Laurens' Hill with a strong skirmish line. He will mass the remainder of his force in front of the works and co-operate with General Wood, protecting the latter's left flank against an attack by the enemy.

"Fifth. Maj. Gen. James B. Steedman, commanding District of the Etowah, will occupy the interior line in rear of his present position, stretching from the [old] reservoir on the Cumberland River to Fort Negley, with a strong skirmish line, and mass the remainder of his force in his present position, to act according to the exigencies of the service during these operations.

"Sixth. Brig. Gen. J. F. Miller, with the troops forming the garrison of Nashville, will occupy the interior line from the battery on Hill 210 to the extreme right, including the inclosed work on the Hyde's Ferry road.

"Seventh. The quartermaster's troops, under command of Bvt. Brig. Gen. J. L. Donaldson, will if necessary, be posted on the interior line from Fort Morton to the battery on Hill 210.

"The troops occupying the interior line will be under

the direction of Major-General Steedman, who is charged with the immediate defense of Nashville during the operations around the city.

"Should the weather permit the troops will be formed in time to commence operations at 6 a.m., or as soon thereafter as practicable."[29]

General Thomas in his report of the battle of Nashville states that this plan of battle "with but few alterations" was strictly adhered to. This sounds innocent enough, but General Schofield (never celebrated for his retiring modesty) felt that it unduly minimized the importance of his own suggestion as to the way in which the attack should be conducted.

"The plan of battle, as published," he writes in his memoirs, "placed my command—the Twenty-third Corps—in the left center of our line, where only a feint was to be made. The Fourth Corps was to carry a salient advanced line, while the main attack was to be made on the enemy's extreme left by A. J. Smith's corps and the cavalry. After the order was prepared I went to General Thomas with a map of the position showing the exact length of the several parts of the enemy's line, and explained to him that the force he had assigned to our left wing was at least 10,000 men more than could be used to any advantage unless for a real attack; and that, on the other hand, Smith's force was not large enough for the real attack, considering the extent of the ground occupied by the enemy on that flank. Hence I suggested that my corps support Smith instead of remaining on the left of Wood. To this suggestion General Thomas readily acceded, and orally authorized me to carry it into effect, but made no change in his written order. The result of this change of plan was that the close of the first day's engagement found the Twenty-

[29] *Official Records,* Vol. XLV, Pt. II, 183-84.

third Corps on the extreme right of our infantry line, in the most advanced position captured from the enemy. ... The 'alterations' were certainly 'few.' A change from 10,000 to 20,000 infantry in the main attacking force may not properly be described as *many* 'alterations,' but it looks like one very *large* one—sufficient, one would suppose, to determine the difference between failure and success."[30]

One other change made in the original plan of battle was to assign a somewhat more active part in the proceedings to General Steedman. Instead of standing idly by, waiting "to act according to the exigencies of the service during these operations," he was assigned the duty of actually firing the first guns in the ground attack, in a feint against the Confederate right to veil the main purpose of the action, which was to turn the Confederate left. This change in the plan was pleasing to Steedman, who had evidently been expecting to remain on the defensive and had been experimenting with the idea of building a series of dams in Brown's Creek to flood the low ground in front of his sector of the Federal line, improving his defensive position.

Commenting on Thomas' battle plan, his admiring biographer, Van Horne, says: "In outline this plan does not depart radically from the type most frequently adopted—a feint to conceal the real attack; but in the details, in the tactical combinations, in the close relation of the various assaults, and in the determination of the strength of the various attacking columns, there was displayed generalship that will bear comparison with the skill of the most famous soldiers of the world. . . .

"Seldom has a battle been fought in more exact conformity to plan than the battle of Nashville, and this is true not only in comparison with the great battles of

[30] Schofield, *Forty-six Years in the Army*, 243.

our civil war, but also in comparison with those of Europe, fought by the great masters of war. The leading features of the plan and of the battle itself were the feint upon the enemy's right and the combinations of infantry and cavalry in overwhelming attacks upon his left, resulting in doubling up successive portions of his line and finally dislodging him altogether. It was unlike the typical battle of the Confederate commanders—massing so heavily against a flank as to forbid a strong general line of battle. Thomas made provision for a strong line of battle throughout its entire length, for overwhelming attacking columns, for a feint which might have been easily turned to a successful turning movement, and for security to his rear in the event of unsuccessful offense. Hood's hope of following a defeated army into the city of Nashville would not have been realized had he repulsed every attack made upon his entrenched army. In these respects and others, the battle of Nashville was distinctive, illustrating generalship which comprehended the minutest details, as well as the grandest combinations."[31]

In connection with his carefully laid plans for the offensive movement of his infantry and cavalry, Thomas had also been closely in touch with the naval forces entrusted with the duty of guarding the river approaches to the city. The Confederates had no serious intention of crossing the river in force and by-passing Nashville on a northward march, but Thomas was in constant fear that they might do so, and this fear was accentuated when Commander Fitch reported to him on December 8 that the enemy had crossed the river below Harpeth. Thomas promptly asked Admiral Lee at Clarksville if he could sent the ironclad *Cincinnati* up the river for patrol duty between Clarksville and the Harpeth

[31] Van Horne, *Life of Thomas*, 322.

Shoals, but Lee replied that the low stage of water made it imposible for that vessel to cross Davis Ripple at the foot of the Shoals and that he had no other gunboat available. Fitch, from his headquarters on the *Neosho* at Robertson's Island, also reported that the low water made it impossible for him to get down the river to Harpeth.[32] So, there was left a stretch of seventeen miles of the Cumberland which could not be patrolled by the gunboats—but this was by now a matter of only academic interest, as Hood had no idea of crossing the river, except with isolated foraging parties. If Hood had known that this unguarded stretch of river was at low water, he might have been able to make some effective use of the information, but he does not seem to have been informed of it.

Looking ahead to the impending battle, Thomas on the thirteenth asked Fitch to co-operate "by engaging the batteries [manned by Chalmers's cavalry] on the river below the city, and thus attracting their attention while the troops are in motion against the enemy's position." Fitch confidently replied that "If the weather and water will permit I will surely give the rebel batteries below sufficient amusement to keep them occupied, and at the same time try to induce them to bring as many guns on the river as possible." The next day Fitch was informed that "the enemy will be attacked at an early hour in the morning. If you can drop down the river and engage their batteries on the river-bank it will be excellent co-operation." Thomas prudently warned Fitch, however, that "It is very probable that these river batteries of the enemy will be attacked in rear by our forces, and it is very desirable and necessary that your fire does not injure the attacking force. . . ."[33]

Meanwhile Hood was by no means idle. He was

[32] *Official Records*, Vol. XLV, Pt. II, 98, 101. [33] *Ibid.*, 170, 182.

acutely aware of the great disparity in numbers between his decimated forces and those of the Federal commander opposing him, and he was desperately making every possible effort to increase his strength.

On December 5 he sent a flag-of-truce letter to Thomas proposing an exchange of prisoners, but Thomas replied that all his captured Confederates had been sent to Northern prisons, so nothing came of that. On the next day he telegraphed Secretary of War Seddon in Richmond recommending that General Breckinridge with his forces "either be ordered into Kentucky or to join this army"—but nothing came of that, either. The effort to obtain reinforcements from the Trans-Mississippi Department was being pushed, but that was foredoomed to failure. Overlooking no opportunity to bolster his thin line, he ordered the Assistant Inspector General at Corinth to "send forward at once" all men belonging to the Army of Tennessee, but this resulted in little or no increase in his manpower. General Roddey and his cavalry in North Alabama were on December 6 ordered to join Hood at Nashville "as soon as possible,"[34] but they never got there.

On December 13 Hood telegraphed Beauregard at Montgomery, asking that Baker's brigade of the Army of Tennessee, then at Mobile, be returned to the main command, as "All the troops we can get are needed here"—a masterpiece of understatement. On the same date he received from his Inspector General the discouraging information that since the army had entered the state of Tennessee the recruits had been disappointingly small in number, only 164 in all. He was also informed that of 296 dismounted cavalry assigned to General Edward Johnson's division, "all have deserted except 42"[35]—it being a notorious fact that a cavalry-

<hr>

34 *Ibid.*, 56-57, 653, 655.   35 *Ibid.*, 685.

man considered it an indelible disgrace to be assigned
to the infantry.

As late as the morning of December 15 Hood was still
striving manfully, though ineffectively, to build up his
meager forces, even ordering the officers of all military
courts to "come forward at once."[36] But even as this
order was being promulgated, the Federal rifles were
beginning to crackle, and the outmanned Army of
Tennessee was being forced into mortal combat with
no more than the sadly depleted forces who had been
shivering in their shallow works for two weeks.

As a matter of fact, Hood was destined to fight the
battle of Nashville with fewer men than he had at the
close of the battle of Franklin, as there were still detached from his main force the two brigades of infantry
and two divisions of cavalry (nearly a quarter of his
total force) under General Forrest himself, which were
operating against the Nashville and Chattanooga Railroad and the Murfreesboro garrison.

Military critics have characterized as one of Hood's
greatest blunders this diversion of Forrest personally,
together with so large a part of his fighting force, to the
relatively unimportant chore of reducing or containing
the Murfreesboro garrison. Deserters from the Confederate forces in front of Nashville, before the battle, reported to their Federal captors that Hood was planning
to capture Murfreesboro and withdraw his whole army
to that point for the remainder of the winter, without
engaging the Federals in battle at Nashville. Hood nowhere makes any mention of any such plan in his official
reports or in his subsequent postwar writings, although
this does not necessarily prove that he did not contem-
plate some such move. It might actually have been an
alternative plan of operation, frustrated by the un-

[36] *Ibid.*, 690.

expectedly strong resistance of the Murfreesboro garrison, which greatly out-numbered the force sent against it. On the other hand, the stories told by the deserters might have been either a repetition of baseless campfire gossip or "planted" rumors deliberately passed on to the Federals by pseudodeserters, a familiar Confederate ruse for confusing the enemy.

At any rate, Hood did seem to have Murfreesboro very much on his mind, and did suggest to Forrest on December 8 that he endeavor to drive the enemy troops back to Murfreesboro "and then give them an opportunity to go out from there either toward Lebanon or any other direction they may choose." At this time it is impossible to determine why Hood may have thought that the Federals would voluntarily evacuate Murfreesboro. He seemed to consider this a distinct possibility, however, and on December 9 directed General A. P. Stewart, on the left of the Confederate line at Nashville, to "push forward, with all possible haste, the work of fortifying the hills in rear of your left upon which you are now working, that you may be in readiness, whenever called upon, to move with two of your divisions and one other division from another corps, with a battery to each of these divisions, to prevent the enemy from re-enforcing Murfreesborough, or to capture the force now at Murfreesborough should it attempt to move off."[37]

Aside from his vigorous though unsuccessful efforts to increase his numerical strength, Hood during the days preceding the opening of active hostilities was alert and active in taking all possible steps to have his command at the peak of efficiency and preparedness, within the existing limitations. It was ordered that regular and frequent roll calls be made as a means of preventing

[37] *Ibid.,* 666, 669.

straggling and that commanding officers have their entire lines examined late each evening and early each morning to observe the enemy and ascertain if any change in their own position should take place during the night.[38]

On the tenth Hood issued a circular order to all commanders, stating that it was "highly probable that we will fight a battle before the close of the present year" and urging that the troops be "kept well in hand at all times." Should the battle occur in front of Nashville, the order said, the corps commanders "when it appears imminent" should send all their wagons, except the artillery, ordnance and ambulances, to the vicinity of Brentwood to be parked there. General Stewart was instructed to "select all good points in rear of his left flank" and to have them fortified with self-supporting detached works "to secure it against any attempt the enemy might make to turn it." General Cheatham was instructed to do the same on the right flank of the army's position. General Lee, in the center, was ordered to "select all good points in rear of his right and left flanks, and fortify them with strong self-supporting detached works, so that should it become necessary to withdraw either of the corps now upon his flanks that the flank thus becoming the right or left flank of the army may be in condition to be easily defended." Hood's idea of the great importance of these supplementary fortifications is indicated by the fact that the corps commanders were specifically urged to superintend these particular activities in person, "not leaving them either to subordinate commanders or engineer officers."[39]

On December 13, informed by his spies of the crossing of the Federal cavalry from Edgefield to Nashville, Hood correctly surmised (or was informed) that they

[38] *Ibid.*, 665.   [39] *Ibid.*, 672.

were destined to operate from the Federal right against Chalmers' cavalry on his extreme left, and he instructed General Stewart to put a brigade, instead of a regiment, of infantry on the Harding pike to support the cavalry on that front and to "give Chalmers such assistance as you think necessary."[40] Chalmers was also alerted to this threat.

As late as the morning of December 15 Hood was issuing orders regarding "the inclosed works which are now being built on the flanks of the army," ordering that they be so pierced for artillery that they might fire in any direction, and concluding: "Positive orders must be given to the officers and men that they are to hold the work at all hazard, and not to surrender under any circumstances."[41]

The same morning General Lee was writing a note to General Stewart, saying that he felt secure in his line and was throwing up redoubts on his flanks as previously instructed. He concluded with the prescient remark: "I think you may look out for a demonstration on your left to-day. . . ."[42] And, even as he wrote these words, the rattle of gunfire to the westward gave evidence that the "demonstration" was getting under way.

[40] *Ibid.*, 686.   [41] *Ibid.*, 690-91.   [42] *Ibid.*, 691.

IV

The First Day of Battle

AT four o'clock on the morning of December
15 the brassy blare of the reveille bugles was heard all
along the Federal lines, and the movements preliminary
to the day's action were set in motion. A heavy blanket
of fog hung over the city and its environs, and there was
a spectral quality to the predawn activities as the troops
began to move to their appointed places.

Thomas himself was up early. The gaslights were
still glimmering dimly in the city's fog-wrapped streets
as the commanding general paid his bill at the St. Cloud
Hotel, checked out with his baggage, and mounted his
horse to ride to the front line of the battle. Thomas had
chosen as his headquarters for the day the high hill east
of the Hillsboro pike which was the main salient in the
Federal outer line of works, as from this eminence he
could have a panoramic view of the surrounding terrain
and watch the development of his battle plans.

As scheduled, the first movements of troops were on
the left of the line, where General Steedman was in
command. Shortly after four o'clock Wood's Fourth
Corps and Schofield's Twenty-third Corps were moved
out of the works into position to take active part in the
impending battle. As soon as they were out of the line,
General Charles Cruft's provisional division of new recruits and others were placed in the works from near
the Acklen place (Belmont) to Fort Negley, commanding the approaches to the city by the Granny White,

Franklin and Nolensville turnpikes.[1] Shortly afterward, General John F. Miller reported to Steedman with the Nashville garrison troops, and they occupied the works from Fort Negley to the Lebanon turnpike on the left, commanding that road as well as the Murfreesboro pike. A little later General James L. Donaldson with his armed quartermaster's force and the other men under his command moved out of their quarters in the city and were placed in the inner line from the right of Cruft's command to the river on the right, commanding the approaches to the city by the Hillsboro and Harding roads. This rearrangement of the force under Thomas provided a continuing defensive line all around the city, while relieving for active combat the approximately 55,000 men who were preparing to move out to take part in the active attack.

Having looked after the establishment of this reserve defensive line, Steedman, at six-thirty, marched out with about 7,600 men to make his scheduled demonstration against the Confederate right. His attacking force consisted of nine regiments of infantry and two batteries of artillery. Three regiments of colored troops were in a brigade commanded by Colonel Thomas J. Morgan; four colored regiments were in Colonel Charles R. Thompson's brigade; and two regiments and a battalion of white troops were brigaded under Colonel Charles H. Grosvenor, acting under Colonel Morgan. The dense fog resulted in some delay in the deploy of these troops, but by eight o'clock Steedman had his force moved into position to launch the opening attack in the two-day battle.

Cheatham's advanced skirmish line fell back before

---

[1] The regiment in position across the Granny White pike was the Seventh Indiana, commanded by Colonel Benjamin Harrison, later President of the United States.

Steedman's opening attack, but the main Confederate line and the lunette occupied by Granbury's brigade held firm. The assault by Morgan's 3,200 men was described by the defending Confederates as "a disastrous failure." Colonel Morgan, in more cautiously chosen words, tells how his successive charges were repulsed and "compelled to withdraw," how "the entire command was withdrawn," later remarking that one of his regimental commanders showed that "he does not possess sufficient courage to command brave men." Colonel Grosvenor, using even plainer language, reported that the Second Battalion "behaved in a most cowardly and disgraceful manner" and "stampeded." Colonel William R. Shafter, commanding one of Morgan's attacking regiments, was described by Morgan as "cool and brave, and a good disciplinarian"; but Shafter in his report was frank enough to admit that "we were soon obliged to fall back, which was done in rather a disorderly manner." Later in the day some of Morgan's men got possession of the Rains residence, close to the Confederate line, and cut loopholes in the house and in the brick outbuildings, from which sharpshooters were able to maintain a fire on the Confederate position which was annoying but had little effect. Colonel Thompson also relates that the 2,000 troops under him, after their preliminary skirmish, "retired to our position in line," apparently content to maintain the *status quo* the rest of the day.[2]

Private Charles B. Martin, of the First Georgia Volunteers, was among the troops defending the section of the line against which Steedman's attack was directed, and he has left a vivid firsthand account of the action, from the Confederate point of view. He tells how on

2 *Official Records,* Vol. XLV, Pt. I, 527, 536-37, 539, 542, 739. In 1898 Shafter was a commanding general of the United States forces in Cuba.

the morning of the fifteenth the Federals massed their artillery in front of Cheatham's Corps and then goes on: "Just as the batteries commenced firing, a body of troops was observed on our right moving in the direction of the rear of our position. When first seen, the distance was too great to tell whether they were white or black; but half an hour later it was known to be a division of negro troops. . . . Seeing that their route of march would bring them across the railroad below the end of the cut, it was decided to make a trap for them, and they were allowed to come on unmolested. . . . When they had moved forward far enough for our brigade to form in their rear, one of the divisions in our works about-faced and the other did likewise and wheeled to the left. We had the negroes in our trap, and when we commenced firing on them, complete demoralization followed. Many jumped into the cut and were either killed or crippled. Not a single white man was seen among the killed. Where were their officers?"[3] The question is a rhetorical one; but perhaps Colonel Morgan's cowardly regimental commander was among them.

The Federal officers who took part in the action against the Confederate right thought that they had led Hood to believe this the principal point of attack, and that he was thus surprised by the power of the flanking movement that turned his left. As a matter of fact, however, Hood had accurately interpreted the movement of Wilson's cavalry on December 13 as presaging an assault in force on his left, and he had immediately sent additional infantry to reinforce Chalmers' cavalry in that sector. Also recognizing Steedman's attack for what it was, a feint, he had begun withdrawing troops from that flank and from his center during the afternoon in

[3] *Confederate Veteran*, XVII, No. 1, p. 11.

an effort to strengthen his left, and Steedman made no further effort to attack Cheatham's weakened position.

Wilson, whose cavalry on the right was to provide the deciding force in the battle now getting under way, handled his part of the assignment with efficiency and a thorough attention to detail. Upon his return from the final conference with Thomas on the afternoon of December 14 he held a little council of war of his own. Assembling his brigade and division commanders, he explained to them that the plan of battle called for them to advance on the right of the infantry, turn and envelop the Confederate left flank, and, if possible, strike the enemy in the rear. In order that there might be no possible misunderstanding, Wilson personally showed each of his subordinate officers exactly the ground on which they were to advance, orally reiterated his instructions, and then supplied each of them with a written copy of the orders.

Wilson's force, now ready for battle, consisted of something over 12,000 men, 9,000 mounted and 3,000 unmounted, organized into three divisions and one extra brigade. During their ten days in Edgefield they had been intensively trained and drilled and supplied with everything they needed in the way of clothing and equipment. The mounted regiments were armed with the new seven-shot repeating rifle, a particularly significant weapon, for it gave them a murderously superior fire power.

Hatch's division was on the left of the cavalry corps, and he was ordered to sally from the fortifications on the Harding pike, with the left of his division connecting with Smith's infantry and its right flank moving by the pike. Croxton had only one brigade, the other two brigades of the division having been sent off to

Kentucky to chase Hylan B. Lyon's Confederate raiders, and this lone brigade was to move out on Hatch's right, conforming to the movement on its left. Johnson's division, of which one brigade was mounted and two were not, was given orders to clear the Charlotte pike of the enemy, keeping in touch with Croxton, and to push on as far out as the Davidson place eight miles from the city, protecting the movement of the cavalry behind it from any counterattack. Knipe's division, with one brigade mounted and the other unmounted, was instructed to move out from the entrenchments on the Harding pike and "advance in readiness to reinforce any portion of the general advance which might require it."

To make assurance doubly sure, Wilson detailed one of his staff officers to each division to see that everything was done in conformity with the general plan. The artillery was ordered to be double-teamed, on account of the soft, muddy ground, and all other wheeled vehicles were to be left behind.

As a final touch to his preparedness, Wilson held a conference with General Smith, with whose corps he was to co-operate, in an effort to plan their activities so as to avoid any confusion in the initial movements of the infantry and cavalry. As suggested by Wilson, Smith promised that when the movement started the next morning he would have General John McArthur's division on his right move to the left by the rear of the cavalry inside the entrenchments, instead of in front of them—but their plans did not work out, much to Wilson's disgust.

As Wilson tells it in his official report: "At 6 a.m. of the 15th of December . . . the corps was ready to move, but owing to the foggy weather and the delay of Smith's corps could not advance until about 10 a.m."

In his subsequently published recollections, Wilson elaborates on the delay caused by what he considered Smith's (or McArthur's) bungling. The dense fog, he says, delayed both cavalry and infantry until 8:30 A.M. When the movement did begin, however, McArthur's division, contrary to the arrangement Wilson thought he had made with Smith, crossed Wilson's front, instead of the rear, and thereby stopped him from moving out with his troopers until the infantry was out of the way. Smith's explanation, as given in his official report, was that "The First and Second Brigades of General McArthur, which moved out by Charlotte pike, owing to the roads diverging widely, and the stubborn resistance of the enemy's skirmishers, he having to silence one battery, did not connect with the main line until nearly 8:30. The cavalry then passed to our right and the movement began about 10 a.m."[4]

Regardless of who was to blame, there was considerable delay in getting the movement under way. Once started, however, it proceeded like well-oiled clockwork. General Kenner Garrard's division of Smith's corps moved out from the works on the Harding pike and passed by the left flank to connect with the right of Wood's corps, which was to serve as the pivot of the big turning movement, as the right wing wheeled to the left. McArthur's division, after shaking off some troublesome Confederate skirmishers, formed on Garrard's right. Smith's third division, under Colonel Jonathan B. Moore, moved out the Harding pike and formed in rear of Smith's center, to act as a reserve to either flank. Once in position outside the breastworks, Smith's corps swung forward, carrying out its instructions to "touch the left and guide right." Thus advanc-

4 *Official Records*, Vol. XLV, Pt. I, 433, 551. Wilson, *Under the Old Flag*, II, 109-10.

ing and wheeling gradually, the corps was soon in a position south of the Harding pike and almost parallel to it. There was some slight opposition from some Confederate skirmishers, but this was easily brushed aside by the greatly superior force of Smith's corps as it advanced in the direction of Hood's left wing on the Hillsboro pike.

The Confederates, of course, had hardly more than a token defensive force between their solid left wing and the river. Colonel Coleman had the surviving remnant of Ector's infantry brigade in breastworks on a ridge west of Richland Creek, north of the Harding pike. Chalmers had the only remaining brigade of his cavalry, Rucker's, on some high ground behind Richland Creek near the Charlotte pike; and Colonel David C. Kelley, with Forrest's "Old Regiment," still maintained his battery of four guns on the high banks of the Cumberland across from Bell's Mills.

Colonel Kelley had been doing good work and thoroughly enjoying himself with his guns on the river bank. He just missed the opportunity to interfere with the transports bringing Smith's corps to Nashville, but he got into action promptly after going into position, and on the afternoon of December 3 captured the transports *Prima Donna* and *Prairie State*. After securing his 56 prisoners and the 197 horses and mules he had captured, Kelley began to unload the cargoes of supplies from the boats. While he was in the midst of this activity that night, the ironclad *Carondelet* and the "tinclads" *Moose, Reindeer, Silver Lake* and *Fair Play* came steaming down from Nashville and recaptured the transports from the cavalrymen. Kelley, however, retained his prisoners and his captured mounts, and he also continued to maintain his guns at this strategic point, keeping up an effective blockade of the river from then until the battle began. During this time Kelley's guns took part in a furious duel with Fitch's ironclad monitor on the river, which was not seriously damaged but forced to retire.

— 2 —

Obviously, Ector's depleted brigade of 700 infantry and its supporting brigade of cavalry could offer little more than a show of resistance to the onslaught of Wilson's 12,000 men, working in conjunction with Smith's infantry corps of nearly the same number. As a matter of fact, Ector's brigade had orders to fall back to the Confederate main line along the Hillsboro pike when attacked, and Rucker's cavalry was operating under similar instructions.

East of Richland Creek, stretching across the Harding pike, Coleman had a skirmish line of two Texas companies, commanded by Lieutenant J. T. Tunnell and Captain House. When, through the lifting mist, Lieutenant Tunnell saw the "vast body of cavalry" pouring out of the Federal works on his left front, with "a large brigade of infantry" advancing directly at his position, he quickly notified Colonel Coleman, who was with the main body of his division behind the creek. Coleman came up to the picket line, sized up the situation, and instructed Tunnell and House "to hold the line until forced to retire, then to fall back over the ridge in order and make a run of about two miles to the Hillsboro pike, where we would find him with the brigade." As the Federals advanced, the thin gray line gave them a volley, and then another and another; but Tunnell relates that "When they got uncomfortably near, we hastily fell back, but in order, over the ridge and then made a run for the brigade" on the Hillsboro pike, as they had been instructed to do.[5]

[5] *Confederate Veteran*, XII, No. 7, p. 348.

The "vast body of cavalry" Lieutenant Tunnell observed fanning out in his front was, of course, Wilson's superb force of mounted men. The "large brigade of infantry" that advanced directly against the skirmish line was really Colonel Robert R. Stewart's dismounted brigade of Hatch's cavalry division, backed up by Colonel Datus E. Coon's mounted brigade. Encouraged and stimulated by the hasty withdrawal of Ector's brigade, Hatch's men thundered on out the Harding pike as far as Belle Meade, moving so swiftly that they were successful in capturing Chalmers' train of fourteen wagons, including his personal baggage, official papers, and records.

Chalmers himself at this time was on the Charlotte pike with Rucker's brigade. General Hood had sent him a message at 2 A.M., warning him that the Federal attack would fall on him in a few hours, and he had proceeded to Rucker's position to take active charge of the cavalry operation in that sector. He complains in his official report that the retreat of Ector's brigade was so precipitate that they did not take time to notify him of their withdrawal, and that the Federals were two miles in his rear on the Harding pike before he knew about it.[6] Coleman's emergency had been so great and so immediate, however, that his neglect of his official correspondence should perhaps not be surprising.

Rucker's brigade had actually had the first taste of the day's hostilities early in the morning when it was shelled by Fitch's gunboats. The gunboats were soon repulsed by Rucker's artillery, however, and he was not attacked by the ground forces in his front until much later in the morning. General Richard W. Johnson, whose division of Wilson's cavalry corps was to sweep out the Charlotte pike, was ready to move at 6 A.M., but

6 *Official Records*, Vol. XLV, Pt. I, 765.

he reported that he was so delayed by McArthur's infantry that it was "about 11 o'clock, as nearly as I can remember," before he was ready to move into action. His plan of operation was to send Biddle's brigade of unmounted men ahead of his mounted brigade, with instructions to dislodge Rucker and his cavalry, who could be seen with its busy battery of artillery on the high ground beyond the creek. The movement of Biddle's men was slow and clumsy, however—maybe because they were unfamiliar with the tactics involved in foot movements, or maybe because they were encumbered with their bunglesome cavalry sabers, which nobody had thought to tell them to leave behind. At any rate, they did not get into action fast enough to suit Johnson, so he instructed Colonel Thomas J. Harrison's brigade to charge Rucker "with all possible energy."[7]

Rucker's resistance was sufficiently stout and tenacious to give his cannoneers time to limber up their guns and move them to the rear; but when the guns had been withdrawn, Chalmers ordered the brigades to fall back to a new position about two miles further out the pike. Here a line was established "along the ridge beyond a little creek which empties into the Cumberland this side of Davidson's [house] and opposite Bell's Mill ... his left resting upon the river and his line stretching some distance across the pike." Johnson, coming on in pursuit, had requested Croxton to bring up his brigade on the left and close in on Rucker's flank. He had also suggested to the commander of one of the Federal gunboats that "by dropping down to near Bell's Mills he might enfilade the rebel line."[8] Croxton, however, had meanwhile been ordered by Wilson to move to his left and close up on Hatch's right, so Johnson waited for

7 *Ibid.,* 599.
8 *Ibid.,* 600. Davidson's house (later burned) was just southeast of intersection of Davidson road with Charlotte pike.

him in vain. The gunboat obligingly lobbed over a large number of its big bombshells which dropped around the Confederate position with ear-splitting explosions, but the shells did little or no actual damage except to some of the civilians' homes in the neighborhood, and Rucker held on to his strong position on the ridge. Johnson made one or two half-hearted attacks but each time was repulsed by Rucker's musketry and artillery fire. He accordingly decided to wait until the next morning before making any further effort.

Chalmers, however, fully realized the untenable nature of his position, and also the importance of getting his force more closely in touch with the main body of Hood's army. Late in the afternoon, therefore, he ordered Rucker to move out the pike another mile to a crossroad, and thence to the Harding pike and on across to the Confederate main line on the Hillsboro road. Kelley and the Old Regiment went along with Rucker; the Seventh Alabama Cavalry was left on the Charlotte pike to maintain a position of observation until daylight. The escort company, under the command of young Lieutenant James Dinkins, was sent directly cross country to the Belle Meade headquarters, with instructions to bring off the wagon train that had been parked there on Harding's race track.

When Dinkins and his company arrived at Belle Meade just before dark, they found that the wagons had been captured and burned and that there was a force of Federal soldiers, some mounted and some on foot, in the grounds around the mansion. Undismayed, Dinkins and his company moved around behind the big barn and formed for a charge. Dashing through the yard, yelling and firing as they went, they stampeded the surprised Federals but in pursuing them encountered another body of bluecoats who quickly turned the tables on them and sent them scurrying back through the Belle Meade grounds.

"The enemy opened a hot fire," Dinkins relates, "and as the boys returned through the yard the bullets were clipping the shrubbery and striking the house. Nine of the enemy were killed or wounded and some fifteen captured. As we rode back, we saw Miss Selene Harding standing on the stone arm of the front steps waving her handkerchief. The bullets were falling thick and fast about her, but she had no fear in her heart. She looked like a goddess. She was the gamest little human being in all the crowd. I passed and caught her handkerchief and urged her to go into the house, but she would not until the boys had disappeared behind the barn. They fell back across the pike and awaited the coming of General Chalmers, who soon arrived."[9]

Late that night, Chalmers, with Rucker's brigade, made his way across the fields and byroads, swinging wide to steer clear of the intervening Federals, and at length arrived on the Hillsboro pike, at about its intersection with the present Old Hickory Boulevard. Here he made contact with the withdrawn left wing of the Confederate army and reported to General Hood.

— 3 —

General Thomas John Wood, who commanded the Federal center at Nashville, had the largest corps in Thomas's army—an aggregate effective force of 16,645, with 13,526 "present for duty equipped." Wood was an old regular Army officer, having been graduated from West Point in 1845. He served in the Mexican War, in which he does not seem to have attracted any particular

9 James Dinkins, *Personal Recollections and Experiences* (Cincinnati, 1897), 247. After the war Miss Selene Harding became the wife of General W. H. Jackson, who at this time commanded a cavalry brigade under Forrest.

attention, and in the years intervening between then and 1861 had lived the monotonous, humdrum peacetime life of a regular Army man. His record in the Civil War had been good, and he was generally regarded as a sound and competent, though not especially brilliant, general officer. He had served with the Army of the Ohio and the Army of the Cumberland since early in the war, and when Stanley was wounded at Franklin he succeeded to the command of the Fourth Corps.

With characteristic efficiency and care for details Wood had assembled his division commanders at his headquarters on the evening of December 14. After explaining the intended movements to them fully, he handed to each of them a copy of the orders of the day for the fifteenth: Reveille was to sound at 4 A.M.; the troops were to have their breakfast, break camp, pack up everything and be ready to move at 6 A.M. General Washington L. Elliott, commanding the second division, was to move out by his right, form in echelon with Smith's left, and advance with Smith's troops when they moved. General Nathan Kimball, commanding the first division, was to move within the lines to the Hillsboro pike, then out the pike far enough to form in echelon to General Elliott's left and move forward when Elliott moved. The third division, under General Samuel Beatty, was to draw out of the works by his left, forming in echelon on Kimball's left.

Wood's orders left nothing to chance or guesswork: "The pickets on post . . . will advance as a line of skirmishers to cover the movement. The formation of the troops will be in two lines—the front line deployed, the second line in close column by division, massed opposite the interval in the front line. Each division commander will, so far as possible, hold one brigade in reserve. Five wagon-loads of ammunition, ten ambulances, and the wagons loaded with the intrenching tools, will, as nearly as possible, follow immediately after each division; the remaining ammunition wagons, ambulances, and all other wagons will remain inside of our present lines until further orders. One rifle battery will accompany the Second Division, and one battery of light 12-pounders will accompany each of the other divisions; the rest of the artillery of the corps will maintain its present positions in the lines."[10]

Wood's men had gone into the designated positions when they moved out of the works early in the morning, with only minor delay, due to the fog. From then until shortly after noon the main body of the corps remained inactive, waiting for the adjustment of Smith's and Wilson's forces on their right. Wood's skirmishers, however, had been pushed forward and soon became sharply engaged with the Confederate skirmish line, keeping up a brisk but deceptive show of action. Since early morning the guns in Fort Negley and the other forts, as well as the batteries in position along the long line, had been thundering their salvos, which had aroused a replying artillery fire from the Confederate positions—all of which, in Wood's conservative understatement, "Added interest to the scene"[11] while he waited.

Wood's reference to the "scene" is a reminder of the fact that the battle of Nashville was fought before an exceptionally large "gallery" of civilian spectators. One of the division commanders in Schofield's corps comments on this distinctive feature of the battle, recalling that "citizens of Nashville, nearly all of whom were in sympathy with the Confederacy, came out of the city in droves. All the hills in our rear were black with human beings watching the battle, but silent. No army

[10] *Official Records,* Vol. XLV, Pt. I, 127-28.   [11] *Ibid.,* 128.

on the continent ever played on any field to so large and so sullen an audience."[12]

At length, about 12:30 P.M., when Smith's wheeling line of infantry had been brought around to a point where it served as a continuation of Wood's right, Wood ordered his men forward. The great wheeling movement of more than 30,000 men got under way, and Stewart's men guarding Hood's left flank knew that the hour of trial had arrived, as they heard what one of the men described as "the sharp rattle of fifty-calibre rifles, sounding like a cane-brake on fire." Wood, in more poetic language, says: "When the grand array of the troops began to move forward in unison the pageant was magnificently grand and imposing. Far as the eye could reach, the lines and masses of blue, over which the nation's emblem flaunted proudly, moved forward in such perfect order that the heart of the patriot might easily draw from it the happy presage of the coming glorious victory."[13]

The swinging advance of the troops threw Wood's third division in front of Montgomery Hill, the salient of the advanced skirmish line in front of the left of the Confederate solid line. From the Federal point of view, the works on Montgomery Hill presented a formidable appearance. In truth, however, the position was but a hollow shell; the only reason it was there at all was that it had originally been selected by the engineers for the Confederate front line, and the breastworks had been thrown up with that idea in view. On December 10, however, Hood had decided that this line was too close to the Federal works, so he had had Stewart move his men to the new main line, which had been established

---

[12] Sherwood, *Memoirs of the War*, 149.
[13] *Official Records*, Vol. XLV, Pt. I, 128.

a half mile to the southward, leaving only a small number of expendable skirmishers in the line crossing Montgomery Hill.

Wood, of course did not know all this, and he had no idea how strongly Montgomery Hill was defended. He knew, however, that it stood in the way of the further advance of his men in this quarter and would have to be reduced. So, after ordering a thorough pounding of the position by artillery fire, Colonel P. Sidney Post, of Beatty's division, was commanded to lead his brigade in an assault on this apparently strong position. At 1 P.M., all arrangements having been made, General Wood gave the order for the men to advance. Then, to quote his official report, "At the command, as sweeps the stiff gale over the ocean, driving every object before it, so swept the brigade up the wooded slope, over the enemy's intrenchments; and the hill was won. . . . Our casualties were small. . . ."[14]

All this time, Schofield's corps had remained idle in the position to which it had moved when it emerged from the works at daylight. The division commanded by General Jacob D. Cox had marched out by way of the Hillsboro pike and formed along that road in the rear of General Wood's right. General Darius N. Couch's division had left the works on the Harding pike, and formed in the rear of General Smith's left.

Cox was an able general officer, although he was without any formal military education or training. He had been an Ohio lawyer and politician, thirty-three years old when the war started in 1861. As brigadier general of volunteers he served first in West Virginia and Virginia and was later with Sherman in his Atlanta cam-

[14] *Ibid.,* 129.

paign. He was in active command of the battle line at Franklin and conducted that operation in a highly efficient manner.

General Couch was forty-two years old at this time. He had been graduated from West Point in 1846 and had served in the Mexican War and in the war against the Seminole Indians. He left the Army in 1855 but returned to the service in 1861. He advanced rapidly with the Army of the Potomac and was a corps commander and second in command to Hooker at Chancellorsville. He was placed in charge of the Pennsylvania militia at the time of the Gettysburg campaign, after which he asked to be retired. He emerged from his retirement in December, 1864, to accept service as a division commander under Thomas, being assigned to Schofield's corps.

While Smith was maneuvering his line into advancing position during the morning hours, Couch moved forward behind his left, keeping within supporting position. Cox's division remained practically stationary, in the rear of Wood and to the left of Couch. As Smith's line advanced he bore more to the left than Thomas had expected; so about 1 P.M. Schofield was ordered to swing his corps far around the rear of the advancing line and form on Smith's right, thus making it possible for Hatch's cavalry to operate still more widely and effectively against the extreme Confederate left. It was late in the afternoon before Schofield had his corps in the position newly assigned to it, but not too late for some of his men to see some brisk action before the day was done.

As Smith's corps advanced after getting into position about 10 A.M., with Hatch's and Croxton's cavalry on his right, his skirmishers drove the scattered Confederate skirmishers before them like a covey of quail, and soon the advancing Federal force found itself confronting the main Confederate line along the Hillsboro pike. The zero hour had come. The unfortunate John Bell Hood was about to reap the harvest for which he had sown the seed.

— 4 —

Hood had not been idle this fateful morning. When it became apparent to him that he was confronted with the overtures to a full-scale engagement, he established his headquarters at Lealand, the home of Judge John M. Lea east of the Granny White pike, and began to do everything he could—which was not much—to meet the formidable assault he could see rolling up on his weakly defended left wing.

Stewart, who soon perceived that his position was the immediate objective of the attack, also began making every effort toward the best possible disposition of his inadequate manpower. When he had moved back on December 10 from the Montgomery Hill line to the solid works he now held, based on his main salient at Redoubt No. 1, Major General Edward C. Walthall's division was not placed in the line but was put in bivouac to the left "in the neighborhood of [Felix] Compton's house" (presently the residence of A. M. Burton about five and a half miles from Nashville). It thereby became the extreme left of the Confederate infantry line. Walthall was the youngest division commander in Hood's army, only thirty-three years old, but he was a dogged fighter of great ability. His division had been in the thick of the fight at Franklin, suffering severe losses; one of his brigades had 432 casualties out of the 1,100 who went into the battle. Upon the departure of General French that morning, his two brigades (Ector's and Sears's) were assigned to Walthall,

Ector being sent to the relief of Chalmers and Sears placed in the main line, to the left of Loring, holding the salient embracing Redoubts No. 1 and No. 2.

As soon as Stewart received word that the Federals were advancing in full strength west of the Hillsboro pike, Walthall was ordered to place his men under arms and prepare for action. He placed a company of infantry and a battery of artillery in each of the redoubts in his immediate front (No. 4 and No. 5), although they were still incomplete. The remainder of his command was put in position behind a stone wall along the eastern side of the pike, extending for the distance between Redoubts No. 3 and No. 4.

In deploying his men behind the wall, Walthall placed the brigade of General Daniel H. Reynolds on the right, connected with Sears. In Walthall's center was Quarles's brigade, now commanded by General George D. Johnson; and on his left was Cantey's brigade, commanded by General Charles M. Shelley, just about opposite Redoubt No. 4. Major Daniel Truehart's battalion of artillery, normally attached to Walthall's division, had been detached and posted in Hood's main line, with the exception of the two batteries (eight guns) placed in the two redoubts.

When Ector's retreating brigade reached the Confederate main line in the early afternoon, Walthall put it in position on his left. Even with this extension, however, Stewart's line on his extreme left flank was still not long enough to cover Redoubt No. 5, and Stewart is guilty of no exaggeration when he says: "My own line was stretched to its utmost tension. . . ."[15]

Realizing that he was hopelessly outnumbered by the attacking force, Stewart appealed to Hood for reinforcements. In response to this appeal, Hood about noon

[15] *Ibid.*, 709.

ordered General Edward Johnson, commanding the left division of Lee's corps, to send Manigault's and Deas's brigades to Stewart's immediate assistance, later sending also the other two brigades (Sharp's and Brantley's) of the division. Stewart was also informed that two of Cheatham's divisions on the extreme right would be sent to his support, and they were soon on the way. Colonel Henry Stone of Thomas' staff later wrote that "both Cheatham's and Lee's corps were held as in a vise between Steedman anad Wood"[16] during the whole day; but apparently Colonel Stone was not very accurately informed as to what actually took place.

— 5 —

The Federal attacking force swept through the wedge of territory between the Harding and Hillsboro pikes like a giant wheel, with Wood at the hub, Smith along the spoke, and the fast-moving cavalry on the rim, moving through the present Belle Meade residential section.

The first collision of the enveloping Federals and the defending Confederates came late in the forenoon, when Colonel Datus E. Coon with his brigade of Hatch's cavalry division found himself on the exposed flank of Redoubt No. 5, the detached and unsupported outermost outpost of the Confederate left. Coon's men quickly dismounted and, with their deadly Spencer repeaters, moved to the attack. They were supported by the first brigade of McArthur's division and a battery of artillery which immediately opened fire on the Confederate position. An artillery duel continued for about an hour, but there were relatively few casualties. Meanwhile Coon's dismounted troopers, as well as the infantry brigade, were gradually moving up closer to the

16 Robert Underwood Johnson and Clarence Clough Buel (eds.), *Battles and Leaders of the Civil War* . . . , 4 vols. (New York, 1887-88), IV, 457.

Confederate works. At length Coon's brigade was ordered to the charge, and the infantry received similar orders. The four Napoleon guns on the hill met the charge with a burst of grape and canister, accompanied by as heavy a musketry fire as the defenders could develop with their single-shot muskets, but the result could never be in doubt. The fast-shooting Federals swarmed up the hill and literally overpowered the defending force, capturing the guns and practically all the men in the redoubt. There was some dispute among the victors as to who got there first. Smith says that Coon's men entered the fortification "simultaneously with our skirmishers"; but the cavalrymen deny this, saying that the infantry did not get there until after they had the situation well in hand.

Whoever got there first, the Federals had hardly reached the inside of the captured works before they received a salvo from the guns in Redoubt No. 4, and they then turned their attention to this Confederate strong point, which was in the process of being invested by the rest of Hatch's and McArthur's divisions.

Redoubt No. 4 proved to be not quite such an easy nut to crack as No. 5, although held by no larger a force. It was defended by a battery of four smooth-bore Napoleon guns, fairly accurate at six to eight hundred yards, manned by forty-eight artillerymen under the command of Captain Charles L. Lumsden, a graduate of Virginia Military Institute who had been commandant of cadets at the University of Alabama when the war started. The battery was supported by 100 infantry under Captain Foster of the Twenty-ninth Alabama, these men being in shallow breastworks stretching for a short distance on either side of the redoubt. They had been ordered to hold their position "at all hazards," and they took their orders literally.

As Ector's retreating brigade came streaming by the redoubt about 11 A.M., Lumsden called out to some of the commanding officers, urging them to reinforce him and help him hold his position. But "It can't be done; there's a whole army in your front" was the reply from Ector's fleeing men, and away they went on down the hill and across the pike to Walthall's rock wall. Then, as McArthur began to shell the little redoubt with three batteries of rifled guns from a ridge six hundred yards to the westward, Lumsden sent word of his perilous predicament to General Stewart, stating that a charge would sweep his men off at any moment. But the best the harassed corps commander could do was send back word to hold on "as long as you can." Battered by that shattering bombardment and almost encompassed by twelve regiments of infantry and two brigades of dismounted cavalry, they could hardly hope to hold on very long.

By some miracle of valor, however, the Confederate defenders did cling to their beleaguered position for more than three hours, banging away with their smooth-bores as fast as they could be served. When Redoubt No. 5 was captured and its guns turned on him, Lumsden ran two of his Napoleons far enough out of their embrasures facing westward to fire to the left behind the left section of his battery. Sergeant James R. Maxwell, in command of this left section, was by this time serving one of the guns himself, taking the place of a wounded cannoneer, and he has left a graphic account of the final scene, the tidal wave of bluecoats engulfing the defenders of the little hill:

"When the charging Federals passed my gun on the left of the redoubt," he says, "Lieutenant Hargrove ordered us to leave it. I ran towards Captain Lumsden's section, where Sergeant Jim Jones had turned No. 2 to fire canister at the Federals who were near gun No. 4. He called to me 'Look out, Jim!'. I dropped on hands and knees whilst he fired that canister right over my head. I took my place between his gun and the embrasure, helping handle the gun, and he gave the double canister charge again. Captain Lumsden was standing with another charge of canister in his hands. The command had been given to fire, but the man with the friction primers had run. I called out, 'Captain, he's gone with the friction primers.' Says Captain Lumsden 'Take care of yourselves, boys.' As he said that, down by my side between gun and embrasure dropped a Federal soldier with his rifle. I left him right there and lit out down the hill. As I got about halfway to the creek at the bottom of the hill, I ran over an infantry man's Enfield rifle. Noticing that it was cocked, with the cap shining on its nipple, I grabbed it up and fired at a Federal soldier who was waving his hat at the guns I had just left."

Later in the evening, when Sergeant Maxwell had gained the relative safety of the Confederate line on the other side of the pike, he relates that "I went down past Mr. Castleman's house, in front of which Captain Lumsden was reporting to General Stewart, who was congratulating Captain Lumsden for detaining the advance of the Federals so long. . . . Hilen L. Rosser, one of our gunners had had part of his head shot away. That night as I was pouring some water for Lumsden to wash, he was picking something out of his beard and said: 'Maxwell, that is part of Rosser's brains.' "[17]

By the time Redoubts No. 4 and No. 5 had fallen to the on-rushing Federals, Schofield had swung his corps around as ordered and was forming on Smith's right.

[17] George Little, *A History of Lumsden's Battery, C.S.A.* (Tuscaloosa, Ala., 1905?), 56.

This made it possible for Wilson to remount his men and move out on a wider arc across the Hillsboro pike, to the left and rear of the Confederate left wing, commanding both the Hillsboro and Granny White pikes. Chalmers being still miles away on the Charlotte pike, Wilson was unopposed as he placed his force in position to take a decisive part in the action on the following day, but he took no further active part in the fighting of December 15.

With the two defending redoubts in Walthall's front wiped out, Smith now subjected Walthall's line to a blistering bombardment of heavy shellfire, to which he was unable to reply, for lack of artillery of his own; but there was no immediate effort to charge Walthall's line.

Walthall had observed with justifiable apprehension the action in his front and the opposition building up there, and he was making energetic efforts to dispose his available force to the best advantage. When Coleman arrived with what was left of Ector's brigade, Walthall put him into position as an extension of the left of his line behind the rock wall, trying to stretch it as far as possible to the south. Then when the flanking Federal force began to seep across the Hillsboro pike, Ector's brigade was moved "down near Compton's house" to hold the pike for the protection of the left flank. When Redoubt No. 5 fell, and the victorious Federals came streaming across the pike, Coleman fell back to the eastward, and a spearhead of advancing Federals drove in between him and Cantey's brigade, effectually isolating Ector's brigade from the ensuing action of Walthall's division.

As the Federals drove across the pike into the woods near the Compton house, occupying the high hill southwest of the house with a battery of artillery, Walthall detached Reynolds and his brigade from his right to his left, stretching out Quarles's and Cantey's brigades into a still thinner line to cover the vacancy left by the withdrawal. In his new position Reynolds occupied a line facing the Federals diagonally across the woods northeast of the Compton house, his right extending in the direction of Cantey's left. Reynolds had some temporary success in stemming the Federal flood, but pretty soon the bluecoats had occupied the hill west of the Compton house also, and were shelling Reynolds with the guns on both hills. As their infantry advanced they threatened both flanks of his brigade and drove him back through the woods toward the Granny White pike. Reynolds, says one writer, "fell back contesting the advance of the enemy with great energy and indomitable resolution,"[18] but his resolution was no match for the overpowering force brought to bear on him.

When Manigault's reinforcing brigade came up early in the afternoon, it was ordered by Stewart to take position parallel to the Hillsboro pike, opposite Redoubt No. 4; then when Deas's brigade arrived, it was placed on Manigault's right to connect with Walthall. These brigades, as well as those of Sharp and Brantley of Johnson's division, operated under the direct command of General Edward Johnson, but they proved to be of little or no help.

The Federals, following up their artillery pounding of Walthall's line, were now moving in on his two brigades behind the stone wall with a massed charge of infantry in large numbers, pressing in from front and flank. Walthall's men had taken about all the punishment they could absorb, and under the relentless pressure of the blue juggernaut they began to give ground, with but little support from their reinforcements.

18 *Southern Bivouac*, N. S., I, No. 3, p. 171.

Stewart in his report says bluntly that the brigades of Deas and Maningault "making but feeble resistance, fled, and the enemy crossed the pike, passing Walthall's left."[19] Walthall says simply that, although the requested reinforcements arrived, "the enemy were not checked"; and that when "Reynolds, bravely resisting, was forced back . . . it was with difficulty I withdrew my other two brigades to prevent their capture by the large force he had been opposing, which moved up in their rear."[20] In short, Walthall, to save his men from capture, was forced into precipitate retreat, and the flanking Federals swept northward east of the pike.

Stewart, seeing the impending debacle on his left, hastily withdrew a battery from his salient at Redoubt No. 1, which was as yet not being hard pressed; placing this battery on a hill east of the pike, he ordered the brigades of Deas and Manigault to rally to its support. "They again fled, however," says Stewart, ". . . abandoning the battery, which was captured. By this time the other brigades of Johnson's division had come up, but were unable to check the progress of the enemy, who had passed the Hillsborough pike a full half mile, completely turning our flank and gaining the rear of both Walthall and Loring, whose situation was becoming perilous in the extreme."[21] Stewart immediately sent orders to both Walthall and Loring to withdraw, and Loring promptly did so, but by this time Walthall's brigades were already in retreat.

Meanwhile, the third brigade of McArthur's division was coming up before that portion of Stewart's position defended by Redoubt No. 3, west of the Hillsboro pike. As the brigade approached the pike, marching across the farmland now crossed by Woodmont Boulevard, it came under the direct and vigorous fire of the Confed-

[19] *Official Records,* Vol. XLV, Pt. I, 709.   [20] *Ibid.,* 723.   [21] *Ibid.,* 709.

erate artillery, which did it considerable damage but did not slow down the advance. When the men reached striking distance of Redoubt No. 3, they were ordered to prepare to storm the fortification, and they immediately moved to do so.

"We advanced on the run down a gentle slope and through open woods until we were out of breath," says Captain Theodore G. Carter of Company K, Seventh Minnesota Volunteers, "when we lay down for a few minutes. Then we ran down across a little brook and lay down under cover of the slope ascending the redoubt. . . . We suffered from the direct fire from the works assaulted, and also from a cross-fire enfilading our line part of the time from the fort on the hill across the pike" (Redoubt No. 1). McArthur's men surged up the gentle slope in front of the work they were attacking, despite the fire of its defenders, and soon were swarming over the breastworks and into Redoubt No. 3. "We had scarcely gained possession of the works," Captain Carter continues, "when the fort across the way [Redoubt No. 2] opened upon us. . . . The gunners cut their fuses so that every shell burst inside of it, and there did not seem to be ten seconds' interval between the discharges. Colonel S. G. Hill, our brigade commander, gave the order to charge the fort on the hill, and was shot through the head the next moment. Our major heard the order and repeated it; we jumped down from the wall and, led by Colonel Marshall, crossed the pike and climbed the hill, the Confederates leaving the fort as we got to it."[22]

— 6 —

The operations against the Confederate left during this eventful afternoon took on some of the aspects of

[22] *Confederate Veteran*, XII, No. 12, p. 585.

a three-ring circus, as one after another of the Federal
bodies of troops successively went into action.

Wood, following his capture of the Montgomery Hill
skirmish line, had recognized that the true key to the
Confederate position was the salient (Redoubt No. 1)
on the high hill in his front, but he also recognized that
it would be a difficult position to carry by direct frontal
assault. The Confederate guns on this hill, Wood
frankly admits, "had been annoying us seriously all
day." Accordingly, he ordered up two batteries of his
artillery and placed them so as to bring a converging fire
on the crest of the hill, the division commanders meanwhile being ordered to push forward as closely as possible. When the Confederate position had been properly pulverized by a half-hour's concentrated bombardment, and when Elliott's and Kimball's divisions had
advanced far enough to occupy some high ground "very
near the enemy's solid works," Elliott was ordered at
4 P.M. to "advance and take the hill in his front"—
Redoubt No. 1. Wood felt that Elliott did not display
the proper alacrity in carrying out this order, and when
he had not advanced by 4:30, Kimball's division was
ordered to attack the salient. "With the most exalted enthusiasm," Wood says in his report, "and with loud
cheers, it rushed forward up the steep ascent and over
the intrenchments," capturing "several pieces of artillery and stands of colors, many stand of small-arms and
numerous prisoners."[23]

What Wood neglects to say in his report is that Kimball's men entered the fortification along with those
from the flanking third brigade of McArthur's division
who had just stormed Redoubt No. 3. Colonel Elliott,
whose division finally got into action along with Kimball, says it arrived there "simultaneously" with the

[23] *Official Records*, Vol. XLV, Pt. I, 129, 155.

men from Smith's corps, but the men in Colonel Hill's brigade tell another story. They say flatly that "Hill's brigade . . . reached the angle of the Confederate line in advance of the Fourth Corps, which was approaching the angle at the same time from the north. *After* the detachments of the 12th Iowa and 7th Minnesota [of Smith's corps] had captured Redoubt No. 2 and were following the fleeing enemy some distance beyond, some of the Fourth Corps entered the redoubt from the north."[24] What neither Wood nor Smith mentions in his report is that, whichever attacking force had the honor of getting there first, Loring's defending force was already in retreat, having been ordered by Stewart to withdraw and form along the Granny White pike.

The last action of the day was on the far Confederate left, where Ector's badly beaten brigade was temporarily cut off from the rest of the army. General Hood, to get closer to the scene of action, had left Lealand early in the day and had taken up a post of observation on the top of a high hill southeast of Felix Compton's house— a hill now known as Shy's Hill, in honor of Colonel William M. Shy, who was killed there the next day. When Ector's brigade, on its retreat from the Hillsboro pike late in the afternoon, was passing this point, they were halted by General Hood. Personally putting them into position on top of the hill, he said to the men: "Texans, I want you to hold this hill regardless of what transpires around you," to which they dutifully replied, "We'll do it, General."[25]

As they formed their line on the brow of the hill, facing westward, they could hear the diminishing roar of the battle along the Hillsboro pike from which they

---

[24] Major David W. Reed, *Campaigns and Battles* (n.p., n.d.), 197-99.
[25] *Confederate Veteran*, XII, No. 7, p. 348.

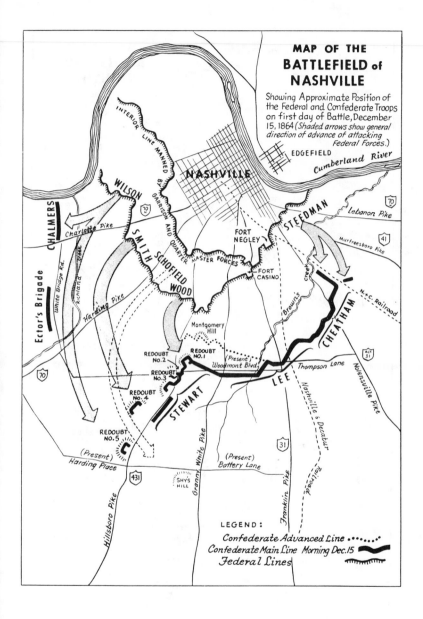

MAP OF THE
**BATTLEFIELD of
NASHVILLE**

Showing Approximate Position of
the Federal and Confederate Troops
on first day of Battle, December
15, 1864 (Shaded arrows show general
direction of advance of attacking
Federal Forces.)

LEGEND:
Confederate Advanced Line •••••••
Confederate Main Line Morning Dec.15 〜〜〜
Federal Lines

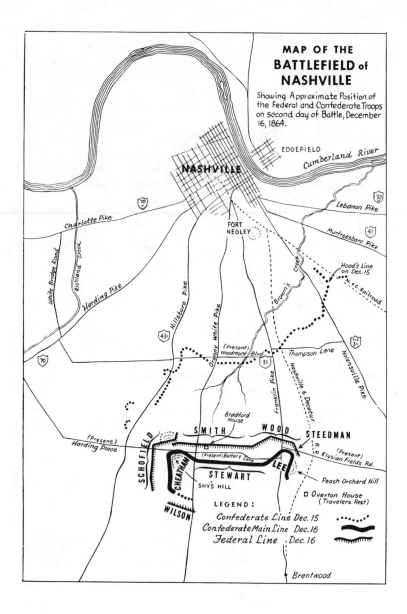

MAP OF THE
**BATTLEFIELD of
NASHVILLE**

Showing Approximate Position of
the Federal and Confederate Troops
on second day of Battle, December
16, 1864.

had become separated. To their right they could see a fresh Confederate division forming a line of battle— Bate and his men, who had just arrived after the long march from the Confederate right flank on the Nolensville pike. Bate arrived too late to be of any assistance in checking the collapse of the Confederate left; indeed, he records that as he crossed the Franklin pike he encountered Stewart's retreating men—"streams of stragglers, and artillerists, and horses, without guns or caissons, the sure indicia of defeat" coming hurriedly from the left.

Unaffected by these signs of disaster, however, Bate pressed on and finally found Cheatham and Hood and was ordered into a defensive position on a hill north of Shy's Hill. The fighting in this quarter was now about over—not quite all over, however, for soon Couch's fresh division of Schofield's corps came sweeping across the Hillsboro pike, eager for action. After a brief but spirited engagement, it drove Bate off the hill he had just occupied. Couch was considering the possibility of launching an assault against Coleman's men to his right, who had beat off a previous attack by some of Cox's men, when the quick December darkness fell, and Couch's force intrenched its position and bivouacked for the night.[26]

— 7 —

As nightfall put an end to the day's fighting, the various units of the two contending armies were scattered across the countryside like pieces of a scrambled jigsaw puzzle.

The Confederate line at this time was in the shape of an irregular zigzag. Cheatham's position on the right had been almost entirely evacuated. Bate was already in position on the left; Lowrey's division was under orders

26 *Official Records,* Vol. XLV, Pt. I, 345, 747.

to follow him; and J. A. Smith's (Cleburne's) division, already on its way to the left, had been overtaken by darkness and forced to bivouac on the Granny White pike near Lealand and Shy's Hill. The two remaining divisions of Lee's corps still firmly held the line in the Confederate center, although stretched out in a pitifully thin line, with his left refused in a defensive manner. Stewart's hard-pressed corps had retired to a position roughly parallel to the Granny White pike, east of that pike and south of the present Woodmont Boulevard, his right resting near the Bradford house on the pike. Ector's brigade clung to its uneasy resting place on Shy's Hill; and during the night Rucker's cavalry brigade took position across the Hillsboro pike at about the point where it is intersected by the road from Brentwood, the present Old Hickory Boulevard. As Stewart's corps fell back that evening, General Sears had his right leg struck by a solid shot from the Federal artillery. He was carried to a nearby field hospital, where his leg was amputated, and he was made a prisoner by the pursuing Federals when left behind at Pulaski a few days later.[27]

One of the dramatic incidents of the battle took place that evening, as the demoralized survivors of Deas's brigade went streaming down the Granny White pike past the Bradford house, in disorderly retreat. Her patriotic ardor aroused by the depressing spectacle, Miss Mary Bradford ran out of the house into the road "under heavy fire" and made a desperate appeal to the retreating men to stop their flight, rally, and fight—but even the anguish of beauty in distress had no deterring effect on the battle-shocked soldiers, who doggedly continued on their way to the rear. Colonel W. D. Gale, assistant adjutant general of Stewart's Corps, wrote to his wife about the incident, saying that "General Hood

[27] *Southern Bivouac*, N.S., I, No. 3, p. 173.

told me yesterday he intended to mention her heroic conduct in his report, which will immortalize her."[28] Thomas' army was also well scattered that evening. On his left Steedman's men held on to the position they had taken early in the day, apparently unaware of the fact that Cheatham had been withdrawing from their front all afternoon. Wood, after sweeping over Stewart's salient, had been ordered by Thomas to move on toward the Franklin pike, reach it if possible before dark, and form his troops across it facing southward. Wood did not receive this order until 5 P.M., about sunset, and by the time he had advanced far enough to cross the Granny White pike it was so dark that he could proceed no further, so he halted his corps about three quarters of a mile short of the Franklin pike, his right resting on Smith's left and his left near the line of the abandoned Confederate earthworks. Smith, after driving the Confederate left wing out of its position, had paused for the night in a fortified line between the Hillsboro and Granny White pikes, nearly parallel to them. Schofield, on the right, was east of the Hillsboro pike, with Couch's division entrenched across the hill which he had occupied late in the afternoon, and Cox's division was on Couch's right, roughly at a right angle to him. Wilson and his remounted cavalry had co-operated with Schofield's corps in the late afternoon in occupying the hills east of the Hillsboro pike, and he spent the night in this locality, on the extreme right of the infantry. Knipe's division of cavalry, closely following behind Hatch, had reached the Hillsboro pike just after Redoubts No. 4 and No. 5 had fallen. His dismounted brigade spent the night in position near that pike, but Hammond's mounted brigade pushed on, by the Otter

28 Bromfield L. Ridley, *Battles and Sketches of the Army of Tennessee* (Mexico, Mo., 1906), 413.

Creek road, to the Granny White pike, where they took a strong position on the ridge where the road passes through a gap just beyond the site of Granny White's tavern.

As his victorious army settled down for the night, General Thomas was making his way back to his headquarters in the city. Here, as soon as he arrived, he sat down and, with what must have been a high degree of pride and satisfaction, penned the following dispatch to General Halleck: "I attacked the enemy's left this morning and drove it from the river, below the city, very nearly to the Franklin pike, a distance about eight miles. Have captured General Chalmers' headquarters and train, and a second train of about 20 wagons, with between 800 and 1,000 prisoners and 16 pieces of artillery. The troops behaved splendidly, all taking their share in assaulting and carrying the enemy's breast-works. I shall attack the enemy again to-morrow, if he stands to fight, and, if he retreats during the night, will pursue him, throwing a heavy cavalry force in his rear, to destroy his trains, if possible." And, ever the dutiful family man, he telegraphed to his wife in New York: "We have whipped the enemy, taken many prisoners and considerable artillery."[29]

Stanton, as soon as he received the news, graciously telegraphed Thomas: "I rejoice in tendering to you and the gallant officers and soldiers of your command the thanks of this Department for the brilliant achievements of this day, and hope that it is the harbinger of a decisive victory, that will crown you and your army with honor and do much toward closing the war. We shall give you a hundred guns in the morning."[30]

Grant also sent a telegram of congratulations, saying

[29] *Official Records,* Vol. XLV, Pt. II, 194, 195.   [30] *Ibid.,* 195.

that "I was just on my way to Nashville" when he received the news, but "I shall go no farther." Then, still generous with long-distance advice, he went on: "Push the enemy now, and give him no rest until he is entirely destroyed. Your army will cheerfully suffer many privations to break up Hood's army and render it useless for further operations. Do not stop for trains or supplies, but take them from the country as the enemy have done. Much is now expected." [31]

The next morning President Lincoln telegraphed "the nation's thanks"; and, taking his cue from Grant, added: "You made a magnificent beginning. A grand consummation is within your easy reach. Do not let it slip." [32]

[31] *Ibid.*   [32] *Ibid.*, 210.

V

The Second Day

THE opposing armies, in their extemporizing of new positions during the night of December 15 and the following morning, were hampered by the unavoidable confusion and the traditional "fog of battle." This was particularly true of the Confederates, as Hood attempted to bring into some sort of effective defensive formation the survivors of the preceding day's shaking defeat. It later developed that Thomas thought it possible, if not probable, that Hood would retreat during the night and that the next day's action would be a pursuit rather than a combat. Apparently, however, the thought of flight did not enter Hood's head; he had no other idea than to take a strong defensive position and invite another attack by Thomas.

Hood's establishment of a new right wing was relatively simple: Lee's corps in the center, which (with the exception of Johnson's division) had been virtually inactive during the fighting of December 15 and had also escaped the slaughter at Franklin, simply fell back for about two miles along the Franklin pike. Here, about four miles north of Brentwood, they formed a line, with Stevenson's division in the center and Edward Johnson's division (which had rejoined the corps after its repulse) on the left, both these divisions being to the west of the road. Clayton's division, forming Lee's right and the right of the whole line, was strongly posted on a hill just south of the present Elysian Fields Road. This hill is referred to in the battle reports as Overton's Hill, presumably because it was located on the Overton property, but it was known locally and by the family as Peach Orchard Hill. General Holtzclaw's brigade, on the left of Clayton's division, was astride the pike, and Gibson's and Stovall's brigades were to Holtzclaw's right, with their lines refused southward along the eastern face of the hill for several hundred yards. For additional protection to this flank, Lee had moved Brantley's brigade over to the extreme right of the line in supporting position.

With Cheatham transferred to the left wing of the army, Stewart's somewhat battered corps was to constitute the center of Hood's new line. During the night Stewart's force was moved back to a new position south of the present Battery Lane, his right connecting with Lee's new line and his left to connect with Cheatham.

Shy's Hill, on which Hood had posted Ector's brigade in the closing hours of December 15, constituted a natural salient for the left flank, and the new line was established on that basis, with Cheatham's corps assigned to this end of the line.

General Bate states,[1] that at about 8 o'clock on the evening of the fifteenth, "Major-General Cheatham came to me and took me with him to find the line I was to occupy. He informed me that he was directed by the general commanding to extend a line of battle from the apex of the hill (now known as Shy's Hill) occupied by Ector's brigade in direction of Mrs. Bradford's house[2] on the Granny White turnpike, so that a pro-

[1] *Official Records,* Vol. XLV, Pt. I, 747-48.
[2] Mrs. Bradford was the widow of Edward Bradford. The house in which she lived, referred to frequently in the accounts of the second day's fighting, stood on the east side of the Granny White pike, south of the present Glendale Lane. The house was burned many years ago, and the present residence of Dr. Harrison H. Shoulders, Sr., stands on its site.

longation of the same would strike the line then occupied by General Stewart. We went together and
found General Sharp's brigade on left of that corps, in
the rear of Mrs. Bradford's house, somewhat parallel
to the turnpike, its right resting near the woods, in
which we were informed the balance of that corps was.
A fire was kindled, by General Cheatham's order, to
indicate the direction of my line from the given point
on the left."

Bate then goes on to tell how he moved his command
into the position indicated, despite the difficulties due
to the darkness and the muddy, marshy fields which
were so deep in mire that the artillery could not be
moved through them. As ordered, he placed his left
near the crown of Shy's Hill, on the slope facing the
Granny White pike, adjusted to the right of Ector's
brigade on top of the hill, with his own right extending
through a corn field, advanced toward Nashville and
therefore not quite at right angles with the turnpike.
His men worked along this line throughout the whole
night and constructed a line of breastworks which Bate
described as "impervious to ordinary shots."

Not until next morning did Bate discover that during the night Stewart's two divisions had been retired
in echelon from Bate's right, with Walthall on the same
side of the turnpike as Bate, and Loring on the opposite side of the pike, behind the stone wall that forms
the northern boundary of Lealand. Bate's line then
stood with Jackson's brigade on the right of his division, in echelon with Walthall on Stewart's left. On
Jackson's left was Finley's brigade, now commanded by
Major Jacob A. Lash; and on Lash's left was Tyler's
brigade, now commanded by General Thomas Benton
Smith. Ector's brigade, on the western side of the top
of the hill, formed a right angle with Benton Smith's

left, and the line was prolonged on Ector's left by General John C. Brown's old brigade (now commanded by General Mark P. Lowrey), occupying the ravine and extending to the hill south of Shy's Hill, with Cleburne's division (now under General James A. Smith) on Lowrey's left, covering the hill and refused to the east, near the present Tyne Boulevard.

Bate says: "The hill on which my left rested was confronted by a similar one within 400 yards and an open field in the intervening valley. On this hill the enemy had planted several rifle pieces during the night. There was a deflection on the left of this, and then a series of hills occupied by the enemy extending to its left and culminating opposite Lowrey's left in an irregular range and greater altitude than those held by us, surmounted here and there by a commanding peak. This range of hills, from the point where Lowrey's left rested, extended at right angles across the Granny White turnpike, almost parallel to and in rear of my line of battle, a distance of not more than 600 yards, with open fields between."

When daylight came, Bate discovered a country road skirting the eastern side of Shy's Hill, and he brought up a section of howitzers under Captain René T. Beauregard (General P. G. T. Beauregard's son) and placed them on "a small plateau making out from the declivity of the hill just in rear of Finley's brigade, from which they could sweep the front of my right and the entire line of General Walthall." This added strength, however, was more than offset early in the forenoon, when Ector's brigade was withdrawn from the line and placed in reserve, making it necessary for Bate to extend his already thin line still further to the left, around the brow of the hill, to connect with Lowrey's right.

From Shy's Hill to Peach Orchard Hill is about two

and a half miles as the crow flies, but the meandering Confederate line was about a mile longer. The new alignment was completed about midnight, and the men worked the rest of the night scratching out the best defenses possible under the difficult conditions and in the limited time available. The morning of December 16 found most of Hood's force exhausted, as would be expected of men who have fought all day and worked all night—hardly the ideal preparation for another day of fighting.

— 2 —

General Hood does not seem to have issued any general orders for the action of the sixteenth. Perhaps such orders may have been written and dispatched but not preserved in the *Official Records;* perhaps the necessary orders may have been given orally; or perhaps it may have been assumed that the officers and men would understand that in the new position they had assumed they would await attack and repel that attack if possible.

From his temporary headquarters "near Lea's house," at 8 A.M. on the morning of the sixteenth, the records show, Hood did send to General Stewart an ominous-sounding message which indicates that he may have had a premonition of the outcome of the day's action. "Should any disaster happen to us to-day," Hood ordered Stewart to retire by the Franklin pike, which Lee was to hold until Stewart had passed to his rear; and a postscript stated that in such a disastrous contingency, Cheatham would move to the rear by the Granny White pike. Presumably similar orders were sent to the other corps commanders. At any rate, Stewart, with his mind evidently on the possibility of retreat, sent orders to Walthall: "Should Bate fall back, keep your left con-

nected with him, falling back from your left toward
right and forming a new flank line extending to hills
in rear."[3]

— 3 —

General Thomas in his official report, after sum-
marizing the events of December 15, states simply: "The
whole command bivouacked in line of battle during the
night on the ground occupied at dark, whilst preparations were made to renew the battle at an early hour on
the morrow."[4] Thomas does not say, however, just what
those preparations were, and there is nothing in the
record to show what general orders, if any, he issued for
the renewal of the battle of the next day. General Cox
does say that General Thomas "held a conference with
his corps commanders in the evening," but none of the
corps commanders has left a record of any such conference—and Cox, of course, was speaking from hearsay.

Wood reports that after placing his corps in bivouac
for the night he sought out Thomas at his quarters to
receive his orders for the next day's operations, and that
these orders were "to advance at daylight the next morning, the 16th, and if the enemy was still in front to
attack him; but if he had retreated to pass to the eastward of the Franklin pike, to face southward, and pursue him till found."[5] Accordingly, at 11:30 P.M., Wood
gave his division commanders formal "orders of the
day" to that effect.

So far as the record shows, General Smith received
no specific orders on the night of the fifteenth, and his
official report merely states that "Night coming on, the

---

[3] *Official Records,* Vol. XLV, Pt. II, 696.   [4] *Ibid.,* Pt. I, 39.
[5] *Ibid.,* 130. *Campaigns of the Civil War,* 12 vols. (New York, 1906)
X, 116.

troops bivouacked in line of battle." Steedman also fails
to report receiving any orders that night; although he
does report that he moved at 6 A.M. on the morning of
the sixteenth "in obedience to the orders of Major-
General Thomas,"[6] not stating when these orders were
given him.

General Schofield goes into more detail, stating that
after darkness on the fifteenth he received an order in
writing from Thomas (not in the *Official Records*)
"which was in substance to pursue the retreating enemy
the next morning," moving his corps out the Granny
White pike.

These orders, Schofield wrote later, "seemed to me so
utterly inapplicable to the actual situation that I rode
to where General Thomas's headquarters were supposed
to be, and there found that he had gone back to his
house in Nashville, to which place I followed him. He
seemed surprised at my suggestion that we would find
Hood in line of battle ready to receive us in the morning, or even ready to strike our exposed right flank
before we could renew the attack, instead of in full retreat as he assumed. I told him I knew Hood much
better than he did, and I was sure he would not retreat.
Finally, after considerable discussion, I obtained a modi-
fication of the order so far as to direct the cavalry to
remain where it was until Hood's action should be
known, and an order for some of A. J. Smith's troops to
support the right if necessary. But no orders whatever
were given, to my knowledge, looking to a battle the
next day—at least none for my troops or the cavalry."[7]

Just how much effect, if any, Schofield's lecture had
on Thomas is not known, and Thomas nowhere mentions the conversation. General Wilson does relate that
he received a written order from army headquarters

6 *Ibid.*, 505.   7 Schofield, *Forty-six Years in the Army*, 244.

that night instructing him to "remain in your present position until it is satisfactorily known whether the the enemy will fight or retreat"[8]—and Thomas did order Moore's division from Smith's corps to reinforce the jittery Schofield.

Schofield's corps spent the night of December 15 in the position east of the Hillsboro pike which it had occupied at the close of the day's fighting. Couch's division was dug in on a line running roughly east and west across the hill facing Shy's Hill. Cox's division was in a north-and-south line, at right angles to Couch's position, facing Shy's Hill from the west and also facing the elevations to the south of it which constituted the refused Confederate left wing on the sixteenth. Both divisions had thrown up breastworks, and Cox had slightly refused the line of his brigade on his right, to guard against an attack from that direction, which Schofield seemed to regard as a distinct possibility. Moore's division, from Smith's corps, had been placed in position to plug a gap that existed between Cox and Couch; so, when day dawned on the sixteenth, Schofield's corps was in position to meet whatever activities developed.

Smith, at daybreak on the sixteenth, advanced his corps cautiously, not knowing just where the enemy would be found. With his first division on the right and the second on the left, he proceeded until he located the Confederates in their new position. "Changing my front by a half wheel by brigades," Smith reports, "the command moved slowly in echelon from the right, so as not to break connection with the Fourth Corps, and took a position directly in front of the enemy at a distance of about 600 yards, my right resting at the base of a hill on the top of which was the enemy's left, and my line, being the whole front of two divisions, extending about

8 *Ibid.*, 264.

one mile [eastward]. . . . The Twenty-third Corps was on my right in the intrenchments thrown up by them the night before, and nearly at right angles with my present line."[9]

The men of the Seventh Minnesota regiment were on the extreme left of Smith's corps, and Captain Carter tells how they marched across a field and into the ravine which led up to the rear of the Bradford house, where they paused to catch their breath as their artillery opened "a brisk cannonading" over their heads. The regiment moved out of this ravine into line of battle "at right angles to the Granny White pike [a short distance north of the present Battery Lane], our left slightly in advance of the house but a little to the right of it, the Twelfth Iowa being between us and the pike. Here we lay in the rain skirmishing until about 3 P.M."[10]

Smith's corps was awkwardly located, with his right directly in front of Couch's position and a considerable interval between his left and Wood's right, but no change was made in his position after he established his line.

Wood, acting in obedience to Thomas' orders, started his corps in the direction of the Franklin pike about 6 A.M. on the sixteenth. Lee's skirmishers were soon encountered, but they fell back to the Franklin pike and then southward towards the new Confederate line. Wood soon had Elliott's division deployed across the pike, with Beatty's division on its left and Kimball's massed in the rear of Elliott. In this formation they moved out southward until they encountered a heavy skirmish line established by Lee about a half mile in advance of his solid position based on Peach Orchard Hill.

[9] *Official Records*, Vol. XLV, Pt. I, 435.
[10] *Confederate Veteran*, XII, No. 12, p. 585.

Wood, finding that his right was too far from Smith's left to effect a connection with him, now brought up Kimball's division to form on Elliott's right; and, to quote Wood: "Thus formed, the entire corps advanced in magnificent array, under a galling fire of small-arms and artillery, and drove the enemy's skirmishers into his main line. Farther advance was impossible without making a direct assault on the enemy's intrenched lines, and the happy moment for the grand effort had not arrived."[11]

Steedman tells that at 6 A.M. "my command moved on the enemy's works, and found that he had evacuated the right of his line in my front during the night."[12]— a discovery he might have made the preceding afternoon if he had been more enterprising. Steedman took the precaution of posting a brigade of Cruft's command in his rear to guard the Nolensville and Murfreesboro pikes and then pushed on out the Nolensville road, feeling for the new Confederate front. At length he took a position between the pike and the left of General Wood, with his right resting on the Nashville and De-catur Railroad and his left on the pike. Here he stood until early in the afternoon, when he was instructed by General Thomas to form a junction with the troops of Wood's command and prepare to assault the Confederate right flank.

The energetic Wilson got into action early on the morning of the sixteenth, and by 9:30 had Hatch's division in motion to take position on the right of Schofield's infantry, with orders to connect with Hammond's brigade of Knipe's cavalry division and "drive the enemy from the hills and push them as vigorously as possible in flank and rear." At first this movement met with such strong opposition from the defending Con-

[11] *Official Records,* Vol. XLV, Pt. I, 131.   [12] *Ibid.,* 505.

federates, hastily bent back into a sort of a fish-hook extension of their left wing, that Wilson sent a message to Thomas (through Schofield) stating that the country in his front was "too difficult for cavalry operations" and suggesting that "if I was on the other flank of the army I might do more to annoy the enemy. . . ."[13] Thomas vetoed this suggestion, however, and soon Wilson's men, fighting dismounted, began to push back the defending Confederates, so he changed his mind about the desirability of transferring his activities to the other end of the line—and it was fortunate for Thomas that he did so.

— 4 —

Thomas had his lines deployed in accordance with his ideas early in the forenoon, but except for intermittent skirmishing and a few scattered attacks, which were easily repulsed, there was no general activity of the ground forces until several hours later. The morning, however, was featured by an exceptionally heavy and continuous bombardment of the whole Confederate line by the superior Federal artillery, particularly severe on the Confederate salient positions at Shy's Hill on their left and Peach Orchard Hill on their right.

Shy's Hill was subjected to a heavy all-day cross-fire from three directions. Batteries located on the side of the hill on Schofield's right took Bate's first brigade in reverse, and the guns in the rear of the Bradford house, on a hill where the Glendale Methodist Church is now located, threw shells directly into the backs of Bate's left brigade. This barrage was supplemented by the point-blank fire of General Couch's artillery, one battery of which fired 560 rounds of shells into the Shy's

13 *Ibid.*, 552; Pt. II, 216. Knipe moved by way of the Otter Creek road.

Hill position during the day, razing the works on the left of the angle for fifty or sixty yards.

Bate was poorly equipped to combat this bombardment. In addition to the battery he had placed on the eastern slope of the hill early in the morning, the indefatigable Major Truehart had brought up four guns and placed them on that side of the hill later. Still later Bate managed to bring up Turner's battery to the crest of the hill within the salient. These few smooth-bore guns, however, were able to make but relatively feeble response to the torrent of Federal fire pouring onto the hill; and although Bate's sharpshooters, armed with their Whitworth rifles from England, made life miserable for the opposing cannoneers, the bombardment went on unchecked all day.

Lee also suffered throughout the day from the guns of Wood's and Steedman's corps, which kept up an artillery bombardment of such exceptional intensity that it was considered worthy of special mention in both Federal and Confederate reports of the action.

"The practice of the batteries was uncommonly fine," General Wood says. "The ranges were accurately obtained, the elevations correctly given, and the ammunition being unusually good, the firing was consequently most effective. It was really entertaining to witness it." The Confederates on the receiving end of this entertainment were equally impressed. General Stevenson describes it as "an artillery fire which I have never seen surpassed for heaviness, continuance and accuracy." and General Holtzclaw, of Clayton's division on the hill, mentions being subjected to "a most furious shelling from three six-gun batteries," saying that "One battery of unusually heavy guns was brought down the pike to within 600 yards of my line." Further in his report he says that "The shelling of the enemy's batteries between 12 and 3 p.m. was the most furious I ever witnessed, while the range was so precise that scarce a shell failed to explode in the line."[14]

Lee, in his withdrawal the preceding night, had brought off all his artillery, twenty-eight guns. These he had distributed among the three divisions of his command, so he was not compelled to submit to this heavy shelling without response. General Wood says, "The enemy replied spiritedly with musketry and artillery, and his practice with both was good. In the progress of the duel he disabled two guns in Ziegler's battery."[15] Lee, however, had only two batteries with Clayton's division, where the heaviest fire was concentrated, and Clayton suffered accordingly.

During the course of the morning and early afternoon the Federals made several "feeler" attacks on the Confederate stronghold on Peach Orchard Hill, but none of them was successful. Clayton, describing one of these unsuccessful assaults on his division by Steedman's colored troops, says that the attackers "suffered great slaughter," and goes on to say: "It was with difficulty that the enthusiasm of the troops could be repressed so as to keep from going over the works in pursuit of the enemy. Five color-bearers with their colors were shot down within a few steps of the works, one of which, having inscribed on its folds 'Eighteenth Regiment U. S. Colored Infantry; presented by the colored ladies of Murfreesborough,' was brought in." Holtzclaw reports a "desperate charge" on his line at 10 A.M. and a "determined charge" at noon, both of which were repulsed. Of the losses suffered by the attacking Federals in the second charge, Holtzclaw says: "I have seen most of the battlefields of the West, but never saw dead men thicker than in front of my two right regiments; the great

14 *Ibid.*, Pt. I, 131, 695, 705-706.   15 *Ibid.*, 131.

masses and disorder of the enemy enabling the left to rake them in flank, while the right, with a coolness unexampled, scarcely threw away a shot at their front. The enemy at last broke and fled in wild disorder."[16]

Hood, apprehensive that the heavy assaults on Lee's position might turn his right flank, shortly after noon withdrew three of the four brigades of J. A. Smith's (Cleburne's) division from their place in the works to the left of Shy's Hill where they had successfully stood off Wilson's first attack, and sent them to Lee's support. Lee in his report, however, says that the reinforcing brigades, although put in position on the extreme right of his line, were not needed and "by order of the commanding general . . . started to Brentwood about 3:30 p.m."[17] And this was just about the time that Wilson's cavalrymen were breaking through the Confederate line on the left, at the position from which Smith's three brigades had been withdrawn.

General Thomas joined Wood on the Franklin pike shortly before noon, approved of his disposition of his troops, and gave him some rather vague instructions: that the Confederates "should be vigorously pressed and unceasingly harrassed by our fire," and that he should be "constantly on the alert for any opening for a more decisive effort, but for the time to bide events." Wood says that Thomas also told him that the general tactics of the preceding day were to be pursued on December 16—to outflank and turn the Confederate left—and that he wished Wood and Steedman to co-operate in putting pressure on Hood's right. Wood, after conferring with Steedman and looking over the terrain, concluded that it would be possible to carry Peach Orchard Hill, in spite of the strength of the position. If this could be done, he logically concluded, "the enemy's

16 *Ibid.*, 698, 705.   17 *Ibid.*, 689.

right would be turned, his line from the Franklin pike westward would be taken in reverse, and his line of retreat along the Franklin pike . . . commanded effectually."[18]

Wood, after a thorough reconnaissance of the position, decided to have the assault made by Post's brigade, of Beatty's division, supported by Streight's brigade, with Steedman moving his two brigades forward on Post's left to participate in the attack. Preparations having been perfected, the assault was launched at about 3 P.M., the brunt of the blow falling on Clayton's division and Pettus' brigade, of Stevenson's division.

A cold rain had begun to fall about noon, but it seemed not to dampen the ardor of the attacking force as it moved forward, with "a cloud of skirmishers" in front to draw the fire of the defending line and annoy its artillerists. "The troops were full of enthusiasm," says General Wood, "and the splendid array in which the advance was made gave hopeful promise of success. Near the foot of the ascent the assaulting force dashed forward for the last great effort. It was welcomed with a most terrific fire of grape and canister and musketry; but its course was onward. When near, however, the enemy's works . . . his reserves on the slope of the hill rose and poured in a fire before which no troops could live. Unfortunately, the casualties had been particularly heavy among the officers, and more unfortunately still, when he had arrived almost at the abatis, while gallantly leading his brigade, the chivalric Post was struck down by a grape-shot and his horse killed under him. The brigade—its battalions bleeding, torn, and broken— first halted and then began to retire; but there was little disorder and nothing of panic. . . . After the repulse our

[18] *Ibid.*, 131-32.

soldiers, white and colored, lay indiscriminately near
the enemy's works at the outer edge of the abatis."[19]

Lee in his official report asserts that the attacking
Federals "were driven back in great disorder" and that
their loss was "very severe."[20] That the loss was indeed
severe seems to have been the opinion of everybody who
witnessed the repulse, and there is apparently substantial foundation for the local tradition that the side
of Peach Orchard Hill, after the attack, was blue with
the bodies of the dead and wounded and that it would
have been possible to walk down the hill stepping from
one blue-coated body to another.

— 7 —

But while this attack on the Confederate right was
being thrown back so handsomely, things were not
going so well on Hood's left. There the line had been
bent backward and stretched almost to the breaking
point to meet the ever-increasing squeeze of the invest-
ing infantry on the front and Wilson's hard-driving dismounted brigades, who had gained the Confederate
rear and were applying mounting pressure as they
pushed over the ridge on which they had gained a foot-
hold.

Even without this pressure from the rear, the Confederate left was none too strong. Shy's Hill was a formidable looking elevation, but General Thomas Benton Smith's brigade, when it stretched out into its new
position on top of the hill taking Ector's place, had
discovered to the consternation of the men that the
works established by Ector's men were improperly located. By some engineering blunder, in the darkness
and confusion of the preceding evening, the breastworks

19 *Ibid.*, 133.   20 *Ibid.*, 688.

were placed so far back from the brow of the hill as to give the defending force a view and range on the front of not more than five to twenty yards. Thus, by this error, the steep face of the hill became rather more of an asset to the attackers than the defenders. This fatal weakness was accentuated by the curvature of the hill and the falling away of the lines from the angle, making it impossible for the defenders to protect the front of the angle with any flank fire. The works were also flimsy, apparently intended to protect only from small arms, and had no abatis or other obstruction to impede the approach of an assaulting party.[21] Bate was upset when he discovered this state of affairs, but it was now impossible for him to do anything about it. The Federals had the front covered by a steady fire of sharpshooters from the surrounding hills, and the men in the salient were pinned down tightly by these sharpshooters and by the tornado of artillery fire which swept them throughout the whole day.

A climax to Bate's discomfiture came when he was notified about noon that Ector's brigade had been withdrawn from its supporting position in the rear of the angle, leaving Bate without any support whatever. Bate remonstrated at this and asked for reinforcements, but Cheatham informed him that not only could he send no reinforcements but that Bate must extend his thin line still further to the left, as it had been necessary to withdraw strength from that front to protect the extreme left, which was in the process of being turned by Wilson.

It was soon to develop that Wilson's cavalry, fighting dismounted and wielding the terrifically superior firepower given them by their Spencer repeaters, were able

[21] *Ibid.*, 749.

to supply Thomas with the difference between a stalemate and a smashing victory. Having recovered from the vacillation displayed earlier in the morning, when he had suggested transferring his corps to the other wing of the army, Wilson soon recognized the decisively commanding position he occupied in the rear of Hood's raveled-out left wing, and he set about capitalizing his advantage with energy and skill.

Early in the morning Hammond had gained firm possession of the Granny White pike at the gap in the ridge, and Hatch pushed his division forward in cooperation, extending from Schofield's right. Croxton's brigade was close at hand, in reserve. Wilson's force now presented a battle line a mile and a half long, advancing diagonally across the Granny White pike inclining toward Nashville and completely in the rear of Hood's left. By noon Wilson's skirmishers, at least 4,000 in number (almost as many as Cheatham had left in his whole corps), had pressed their way slowly up the wooded hills in a curving line from the right of Schofield's corps, to a line on the hills parallel with Hood's main line and facing Nashville.[22] Here they were looking down at the backs of Bate's and Walthall's men—a lethal weapon aimed directly at Hood's point of greatest weakness.

Ector's brigade, which had been hurried at double-quick time to Bate's rear and left to form a front on a hill east of the Granny White pike, served as a stumbling block in Wilson's way on that side of the road, helping resolutely to hold this hill until the ultimate collapse of the whole Confederate line late in the afternoon. About 3 P.M. Reynolds' brigade was withdrawn from Walthall's line and sent to the rear to co-operate

22 Wilson, *Under the Old Flag*, II, 115.

with Coleman, and these two brigades held their position so firmly that Wilson's flanking attack was largely west of the pike.

Battered by the continuing artillery fire, faced in front and flank by two corps of infantry, and seeing the flanking cavalrymen pouring over the hills in their rear, Cheatham's men were in a desperate plight. The jaws of the Federal vise were closing relentlessly on them. In the words of one of the luckless Confederate privates caught in this trap: "The Yankee bullets and shells were coming from all directions, passing one another in the air."

"About this time," says Bate in his official report, "the brigade on the extreme left of our infantry line of battle was driven back, down the hill into the field in my rear, and the balls of the enemy were fired into the backs of (killing and wounding) my men. The lines on the [west] . . . of Granny White pike at this juncture were the three sides of a square, the enemy shooting across the two parallel lines. My men were falling fast. I saw and fully appreciated the emergency, and passed in person along the trenches in the angle built by Ector's brigade, where I had placed troops who I knew to be unsurpassed for gallantry and endurance, and encouraged them to maintain their places. The men saw the brigade on the left of our line of battle give way and the enemy take its place on the hills in my rear, yet they stood firm and received the fire from three directions with coolness and courage."

The "brigade on the left" was Govan's, the lone brigade of Smith's (Cleburne's) division that had been left behind when Smith and his other three brigades were sent to the right to reinforce Lee. Both General Govan and his next ranking colonel were wounded and disabled about noon, and this single brigade, attempting to cover the front originally assigned a division, broke and gave ground under Wilson's pressure. Maney's brigade (commanded by Colonel Hume R. Feild) of Lowrey's division was hastily switched over to the gap left by Govan's withdrawal, and the defensive line was temporarily restored.

"About 4 p.m.," Bate continues, "the enemy with heavy force assaulted the line near the angle, and carried it at that point where Ector's brigade had built the light works, which were back from the brow of the hill and without obstructions; not, however, until the gallant and obstinate Colonel [William M.] Shy[23] and nearly half of his brave men had fallen, together with the largest part of the three right companies of the Thirty-seventh Georgia, which regiment constituted my extreme left. When the breach was made, this command —the consolidated fragments of the Second, Tenth, Fifteenth, Twentieth, Thirtieth, and Thirty-seventh Tennessee Regiments—still contested the ground, under Major [H. C.] Lucas, and, finally, when overwhelming numbers pressed them back, only sixty-five of the command escaped, and they not as a command, but individuals. The command was nearly annihilated, as the official reports of casualties show. Whether the yielding of gallant and well-tried troops to such pressure is reprehensible or not, is for a brave and generous country to decide."

Caught between the assault of McArthur's men in their front and Wilson's men in their rear, with Schofield's corps closing the box on the west, Bate's men in the salient were simply crushed as in a nutcracker. Many fled to safety, but many others stayed resolutely in the line and never stopped firing until surrounded and

23 Colonel William M. Shy was only 25 years old at the time of his death. The hill he so bravely defended now bears his name.

captured. Among these were General Thomas Benton Smith and Major Jacob A. Lash, now commanding Finley's brigade. In fact, all three of Bate's brigade commanders were captured, as General H. R. Jackson was made a prisoner as he attempted to make his way back from the front line to where his horse had been left.

"The breach once made," Bate continues, "the lines lifted from either side as far as I could see almost instantly and fled in confusion. . . . I first sought to rally the men and form line in the wooded bottom in rear of Strahl's brigade, Lowrey's right, but found it yielding to the example on its right (there being no pressure of consequence either on its front or that of my extreme left), and hence it was impossible to do so. I was then directed by General Cheatham to form a line at Lea's house on opposite side of Granny White turnpike, but found on getting there that our lines on that flank had also given way, and the enemy already commanding it with his small-arms. The men then, one by one, climbed over the rugged hills in our rear and passed down a short valley which debouched into the Franklin turnpike."[24]

Colonel Henry Stone of Thomas' staff, who was an exultant witness to this history-making event, has written: "It was more like a scene in a spectacular drama than a real incident in war. The hillside in front, still green, dotted with the boys in blue swarming up the slope; the dark background of high hills beyond; the lowering clouds; the waving flags; the smoke slowly rising through the leafless tree-tops and drifting across the valleys; the wonderful outburst of musketry; the ecstatic cheers; the multitude racing for life down into the valley below—so exciting was it all that the lookers-on instinctively clapped their hands as at a brilliant and

24 *Official Records,* Vol. XLV, Pt. I, 749-50.

successful transformation scene, as indeed it was. For in those few minutes an army was changed into a mob, and the whole structure of the rebellion in the Southwest, with all its possibilities, was utterly overthrown."[25]

Hood at the time of the break was seated on his horse on the grounds of the Lealand estate, not far in the rear of Bate's line. He says he was surprised at the sudden collapse of the line, "as our forces up to that moment had repulsed the Federals at every point and were waving their colors in defiance, crying out to the enemy, 'Come on, come on!' " Hood even asserts that "just previous to this fatal occurrence" he was so confident of the day's success that he "had matured the movement for the next morning," which was to withdraw his entire force during the night and attack Thomas' exposed right flank, which was "in the air."

But Hood was rudely roused from this reverie when he witnessed the collapse of his whole left wing, and, as he sadly says, "I beheld for the first and only time a Confederate army abandon the field in confusion."[26]

— 8 —

As the Federals' successful assault on the Confederate position on Shy's Hill was the decisive factor in this decisive battle, it was interesting and instructive to examine the record of what took place in this climactic action as recounted by those who took part in it. These participants' recollections of details are sometimes at variance, but collectively they give a remarkably graphic and detailed picture of this action and the preliminary preparations leading up to it.

[25] Johnson and Buel (eds.), *Battles and Leaders of the Civil War*, IV, 464.
[26] Hood, *Advance and Retreat*, 302.

General Thomas' statement in his official report is notably restrained and terse. He says simply: "Immediately following the effort of the Fourth Corps [the unsuccessful attack on Peach Orchard Hill], Generals Smith's and Schofield's commands moved against the enemy's works in their respective fronts, carrying all before them, irreparably breaking his line in a dozen places, and capturing all his artillery and thousands of prisoners, among the latter four general officers. Our loss was remarkable small, scarcely mentionable. All of the enemy that did escape were pursued over the tops of Brentwood and Harpeth Hills. General Wilson's cavalry, dismounted, attacked the enemy simultaneously with Schofield and Smith, striking him in reverse, and gaining firm possession of the Granny White pike, cut off his retreat by that route."[27]

This colorless, condensed summary of what took place on Shy's Hill greatly over-simplifies the action there. Characteristically, Thomas in his report seems to be making a studied effort to give credit and praise to all who participated, finding fault with nobody. In Van Horne's biography of Thomas, however, there is a much more elaborate account of the events leading up to the action, and as this was undoubtedly inspired by Thomas himself, it is especially significant and enlightening:

"General Thomas rode to the six-mile post on the

---

[27] *Official Records,* Vol. XLV, Pt. I, 40. Actually, three, rather than four, general officers were captured in this action: Major General Edward Johnson and Brigadier Generals Henry Rootes Jackson and Thomas Benton Smith. Colonel Edmund W. Rucker, who was wounded and captured, commanded a brigade but was not a brigadier general. During Hood's retreat from Nashville, the Federals captured at Franklin Brigadier General William A. Quarles, who had been wounded and hospitalized there; and at Pulaski they captured Brigadier General Claudius W. Sears, who had been wounded at Nashville and could not travel beyond Pulaski.

Hillsboro turnpike [about at its present intersection with Harding Place] and met General Wilson between 9 and 10 A.M. Wilson was then endeavoring to carry out the original plan of battle, by making efforts to gain the rear of the enemy's line of battle, but meeting stronger opposition than he had anticipated, he suggested to General Thomas that the cavalry should be transferred to operate against Hood's right flank. General Thomas, however, directed him to continue his movement as already begun until he found it impracticable to attain the end in view, in which event the cavalry corps might be moved to the opposite flank. Wilson then reinforced Hatch's and Hammond's dismounted skirmishers and by noon reached the rear of Hood's left flank. The attainment of this position by Wilson was to be the signal for a general attack from right to left, Wilson and Schofield to take the initiative in conjunction.

"When the cavalry at noon had gained position in the rear of Hood's left flank, Wilson sent a messenger to inform Generals Thomas and Schofield that he was ready to move against the enemy. Schofield, however, did not advance, but at 1 P.M. requested reinforcements. General Thomas was so anxious that the prescribed co-operative attack should be made that at first he directed General Smith to send another division to Schofield. But when Smith protested against being left close to the enemy with only one division, Thomas sent General Whipple, his chief of staff, to ascertain if Schofield needed reinforcements. General Whipple having reported that it was not necessary to take a second division from Smith, General Thomas revoked the order that one should be sent.

"In the meantime General Wilson, being very impatient at the delay of Schofield, sent one staff officer after another to Thomas to make known his readiness to attack, and finally rode round the left of Hood's line to learn the cause of the failure of the infantry to attack.

"At 3 P.M. Generals Wood and Steedman, weary of waiting, attacked Hood's right flank on Overton Hill, with Post's and Thompson's brigades, supported by Streight's. This assault, though vigorous and well sustained, was unsuccessful except in causing General Hood to send troops to his right from his center and left.[28]

"After this action on his left, General Thomas rode towards his right flank to hasten if possible the cooperative attack by Schofield and Wilson. As he reached the position of the Sixteenth Corps, Smith referred to him a request from General McArthur for permission to assault the salient in Hood's line directly in front of Couch's division of the Twenty-third Corps. Thomas said: 'No; the prescribed order of attack gives the initiative to General Schofield in conjunction with the cavalry, and I desire the maintenance of this order; I will ride to General Schofield's position and hasten his attack.' When he met Schofield he directed him to advance against the fortified position in his front. Schofield was reluctant to move from fear of the loss such an assault would produce, and Thomas said: 'The battle must be fought, if men are killed.'

"While the matter was under discussion, Thomas looked to the left and, observing that McArthur was moving upon the angle in the enemy's line, said to General Schofield: 'General Smith is attacking without waiting for you; please advance your entire line.' At this moment General Wilson called the attention of the commanding general to the movement of the cavalry

28 In truth, it had no such effect. Hood had already sent Cleburne's division to Lee's support before the attack, and did not send any reinforcements from his center.

upon the fortified hill on the extreme flank of Hood's line. Both assaults were successful and almost at the same instant McArthur's division, moving southward, carried the angle of Hood's line, and Wilson's troops, moving in the opposite direction and striking the enemy in reverse, gained the other important position."[29]

Schofield has left two accounts of this phase of the battle, one in his official report and one in his subsequently published reminiscences, placing himself in both in a much more favorable light and mentioning in neither any "prescribed order of attack." On the contrary, he says in his memoirs: "The whole forenoon was passed by me in impatient anxiety and fruitless efforts to get from General Thomas some orders or authority that would enable us all to act together—that is, the cavalry and the two infantry corps on the right.

"At length," Schofield continues, "the cavalry, without orders from General Thomas, had worked well round on the enemy's left so as to threaten his rear; I had ordered Cox, commanding my right division, to advance his right in conjunction with the movement of the cavalry and at the proper time to attack the left of the enemy's intrenchments covering the Granny White pike, and that movement had commenced; while, having been informed by General Darius N. Couch, commanding my left division, that one of Smith's divisions was about to assault, I had ordered Couch to support that division, which movement had also commenced. Then General Thomas appeared near our right, where I stood watching these movements. This, about four o'clock P.M., was the first time I had seen or heard from General Thomas during that day. He gave no order, nor was there time to give any. The troops were already in

29 Van Horne, *Life of Thomas*, 330-32.

motion, and we had hardly exchanged the usual saluta-
tions when shouts to our left announced that Mc-
Arthur's division of Smith's corps had already carried
the enemy's work in its front, and our whole line advanced and swept all before it."[30]

Schofield's official report of the battle, which was
written within about two weeks of the event, does not
include the animadversions on Thomas set forth in his
book, written in 1897. Concerning the events of December 16, he says in his report:

"During the morning . . . our operations were limited
to preparations for defense and co-operation with the
cavalry, which was operating to strike the Granny White
pike in rear of the enemy. About noon . . . I ordered
General Cox to advance in conjunction with the cavalry
and endeavor to carry a high wooded hill beyond the
flank of the enemy's intrenched line, and overlooking
the Granny White pike. The hill was occupied by the
enemy in considerable force, but was not intrenched.
My order was not executed with the promptness or
energy which I had expected, yet, probably, with as
much as I had reason to expect, considering the attenuated character of General Cox's line and the great distance and rough ground over which the attacking force
had to move. The hill was, however, carried by General
Wilson's cavalry (dismounted) whose gallantry and
energy on that and other occasions, which came under
my observation, cannot be too greatly praised. Almost
simultaneously with this attack on the extreme right
the salient hill in front of General Couch was attacked
and carried by General Smith's troops, supported by a
brigade of General Couch's division, and the fortified
hill in front of General Cox, which constituted the extreme flank of the enemy's intrenched line, was attacked

[30] Schofield, *Forty-six Years in the Army*, 245-46.

and carried by Colonel Doolittle's brigade of General
Cox's division. . . . These several successes, gained almost simultaneously, resulted in a complete rout of the
enemy."[31]

Cox's version of his division's part in the day's proceedings is slightly at variance with that of his commanding general and makes no mention of any order
he failed to execute successfully. His report states that
Stiles's brigade of his division was ordered to be prepared "to second the movement of dismounted cavalry
toward the enemy's position beyond my right flank,"
but he says that "Schofield did not think it wise to assault the heavy work in front of Cox's division, except
in connection with a general advance."[32]

Cox's suggestion that Schofield was reluctant to attack
seems to represent accurately his frame of mind that
morning. Couch had been keeping Schofield closely
advised of the situation on his front: early in the morning he forwarded information that the Confederates
were fortifying their position; about noon he sent a
message saying that he felt that he might take Shy's Hill,
although he was not sure he could hold it; a little later
he sent word that "the enemy is not in heavy force on
Smith's front." Still Schofield showed no eagerness to
move to the attack. As late as 1:30 P.M. he sent a message
to Thomas, saying "I have not attempted to advance
my main line to-day, and do not think I am strong
enough to do so."[33]

So, Cox says, there was no order given for a general
advance until about 4:30 P.M., "when the cavalry on the
extreme right had pushed past the enemy's left flank."

Cox relates that Doolittle's brigade of his division,

[31] *Official Records*, XLV, Pt. I, 346.
[32] *Campaigns of the Civil War*, X, 119.
[33] *Official Records*, Vol. XLV, Pt. II, 215, 216.

supported by the brigades of Stiles and Casement, was then "ordered to assault the salient on his front as soon as the conical hill in front of Major-General Smith's left [Shy's Hill] should be carried. . . . About 4:30 General Smith's line was seen to reach the summit of the conical hill, and Doolittle was ordered to charge. This he did in the most gallant manner. . . . The enemy was manifestly disconcerted. Their fire was too high, and did no injury to our troops as they scaled the rocky hill. Stiles was promptly up, and as the whole line went forward the enemy broke in confusion, making the best of their way across the hills toward the Franklin pike."[34] Schofield's men, moving eastward to the Granny White pike, met Smith's forces moving southward at right angles to them, and the two commands halted to prevent confusion of the organizations. Hood's left wing had ceased to exist.

Wilson's account of his part in the day's operations is written in his usual brisk and colorful style. After telling of his success in getting his dismounted troopers squarely in the rear of the Confederate left, he says: "In the midst of the heaviest fighting, one of our detachments captured a courier from Hood, carrying a dispatch to Chalmers, directing him 'for God's sake to drive the Yankee cavalry from our left and rear or all is lost.' Regarding this dispatch as of the first importance, I sent it at once to Thomas without even making a copy of it. Having already informed both Thomas and Schofield by courier of my success and of the steady progress my troopers were making, I sent three staff

[34] *Ibid.*, Pt. I, 407. It is understandable that they were disconcerted; the main salient on their right had been carried, Wilson's flanking force was charging into their rear, and three brigades of infantry were assaulting their front.

officers, one after the other, urging Schofield to attack the enemy in front and finish up the day's work with victory. But nothing whatever was done as yet from the right of the infantry line to support my movement. Finally, fearing that nothing would be done and that night would come on again before the enemy could be shaken out of his position by the efforts of the dismounted cavalry alone, I rode around the enemy's left flank to Thomas's headquarters, which I found on the turnpike about two miles from my own. This was between three and four o'clock, and as it was a cloudy, rainy day, it was already growing dark.

"Thomas and Schofield were standing together on the reverse side of a small hill, over the top of which the enemy's line on a still higher elevation could be plainly seen less than a mile away. What was of still more importance was that my dismounted men, with their guidons fluttering in the air, flanked and covered by two batteries of horse artillery, were in plain sight moving against the left and rear of the enemy's line. Shots from their batteries, aimed too high and passing over the enemy's heads, were falling in front of Schofield's corps. And yet he gave no orders to advance.

"Pointing out the favorable condition of affairs, I urged Thomas, with ill-concealed impatience, to order the infantry forward without further delay. Still the stately chieftain was unmoved. Apparently doubting that the situation could be as I represented it, he lifted his field glasses and coolly scanned what I clearly showed him. It was a stirring sight, and gazing at it as I thought with unnecessary deliberation, he finally satisfied himself. Pausing only to ask me if I was sure that the men entering the left of the enemy's works above us were mine, and receiving the assurance that I was dead certain of it, he turned to Schofield and as calmly as if on parade directed him to move to the attack with his entire corps.

"Fully realizing that the crisis was now on, I galloped as rapidly as my good gray, Sheridan, could carry me back to my own command, but when I reached its front the enemy had already broken and was in full but disorderly retreat by the only turnpike left in his possession. This was shortly after 4 P.M. The dismounted troopers had closed in upon the enemy's entrenchments and entered them from the rear before the infantry reached them in front. . . . It was now raining heavily, mist was gathering, and dark was closing down like a pall over both victor and vanquished."[35]

Since it was the men from one of General A. J. Smith's divisions who actually stormed the Confederate position on Shy's Hill, Smith's own detailed report of the action is of particular interest. After telling how on the morning of December 16 he had moved his corps into its new position "directly in front of the enemy at a distance of about 600 yards," with his right in front of Shy's Hill, he continues: "The Twenty-third Corps was on my right. . . . Expecting that corps to take the initiative, as they were on the flank of the enemy, I held the command in its present position, keeping up a slow artillery fire at their lines without eliciting any reply. . . .

"About 3 p.m. General McArthur sent word that he could carry the hill on his right [Shy's Hill] by assault. Major-General Thomas being present, the matter was referred to him, and I was requested to delay the movement until he could hear from General Schofield, to whom he had sent. General McArthur, not receiving

35 Wilson, *Under the Old Flag*, II, 115.

any reply, and fearing that if the attack should be longer
delayed the enemy would use the night to strengthen
his works, directed the First Brigade, Col. W. L. Mc-
Millen, Ninety-fifth Ohio Infantry, commanding, to
storm the hill, on which was the left of the enemy's line,
and the Second and Third Brigades of the division to
attack in front when the First should be half-way up the
hill. Accordingly, Colonel McMillen formed his brigade
. . . and gave his men orders not to cheer or fire a shot
until the works should be gained. Throwing out a
strong party of skirmishers, under a rapid fire from
them and his artillery, he commenced the ascent. He
had no sooner commenced his movement than the Second Brigade . . . took up the attack, immediately followed [by] the Third Brigade, and, lastly, the Second
Division. The enemy opened with a fierce storm of
shell, canister, and musketry, sadly decimating the ranks
of many regiments, but nothing save annihilation could
stop the onward progress of that line. Sweeping forward,
the right of the line up the hill and the left through
mud and over walls, they gained the enemy's works, calling forth the remark from one of their general officers
that 'powder and lead were inadequate to resist such a
charge.' The enemy were whipped, broken, and demoralized. Prisoners were taken by the regiment and
artillery by batteries." An informative feature of General McArthur's report, giving some indication of the
severity of the action, is his statement that during the
two days' fighting his division expended 84,000 rounds
of musketry ammunition and 4,681 rounds of artillery
ammunition.[36]

The rather loose and informal nature of the Federal
action on the sixteenth is indicated by the fact that Gen-

[36] *Official Records*, Vol. XLV, Pt. I, 435, 440.

eral McArthur appears to have acted entirely on his own initiative and without specific orders in making the charge. As he explains it in his report, he consulted with Couch at about 3 P.M. and found that Couch had no orders to advance. McArthur then decided to act on his own responsibility, sending word to his superior officer, General Smith, that unless he received orders to the contrary he was going to make the assault. Smith gave no such orders, and so McArthur went ahead with his privately initiated movement, ordering McMillen simply to "take that hill."

After receiving this order, Colonel McMillen relates, "I immediately withdrew my skirmishers, retired the regiments, and moved them by the right flank to a point opposite the hill to be carried, forming in two lines outside of the works occupied by and in front of Couch's division."

Making these tactical arrangements and procuring additional ammunition for his supporting artillery occasioned some delay, but McMillen at 3:30 ordered his artillery to open fire on the Confederate position and, under cover of this barrage, advanced to the assault, "silently, with fixed bayonets." The brigade had been formed for the assault under cover of the small hill to the north of Shy's Hill; then "Quickly and steadily the brigade moved down one hill and up the other to within a few feet of the enemy's parapet, where we received a volley, which on the right went over our heads, but on the left punished the Tenth Minnesota severely. Nothing daunted, this gallant regiment, together with the others composing the front line, cleared the enemy's works with a bound. The two regiments in the second line were inside almost as quickly, having pushed forward with the highest spirit and determination. Brigadier-General [Thomas Benton] Smith,[37] 84 field, staff, and line officers and 1,533 enlisted men were captured in this charge. . . . "[38]

Further evidence of the rather haphazard, though highly effective, nature of the Federal action on December 16 is supplied by the fact that the culminating assault on Shy's Hill by McMillen's brigade seems to have come as a complete surprise to the rest of the Federal forces, even to those comprising Smith's own left. Indeed, the regiments of Smith's corps east of the Granny White pike had just received orders to entrench for the night and were in the act of digging in when their officers observed the successful attack on their right and then ordered the men east of the pike to charge the Confederate positions in their own front.[39]

As a matter of fact, the collapse of the defenders of Shy's Hill took even Bate's brigades on his own right by surprise. Charles B. Martin, a member of the First

[37] While being marched to the rear under guard, General Smith was (for no ascertainable reason) struck over the head three times with a saber by a Federal officer. Although his wounds were at first thought fatal, he recovered sufficiently to be taken to Fort Warren, where he remained a prisoner until the end of the war. A few years after his return to Tennessee, the effects of the injury to his brain caused him to be committed to the Tennessee State Hospital for the Insane, where he remained until his death in 1923. The identity of General Smith's assailant has never been officially determined. It is stated in *History of the Twentieth Tennessee Regiment* (Nashville, 1904, p. 397), that Smith was the victim of Brigadier General James Winning McMillan, but this cannot be true, as General McMillan was in West Virginia at the time. It is elsewhere stated that Smith was struck by "a Yankee Colonel named W. S. McMillen," but there was no colonel of that name in the army at that time. The only field officer bearing the name of either McMillan or McMillen present at the battle of Nashville was the Colonel William L. McMillen who commanded the brigade of McArthur's division which charged Shy's Hill and captured General Smith.

[38] *Official Records*, Vol. XLV, Pt. I, 442.   [39] *Ibid.*, 470.

Georgia Volunteers of General H. R. Jackson's brigade, was having a pleasantly easy time of it when the blow fell. The ground in front of Jackson's brigade, he relates, was so rough that no assault was made on them, "although our pickets had a lively time with the enemy." Jackson's men were watching with keen interest the destructive effect of the Federal bombardment of Stewart's stone wall across the road, and Martin was seated on the edge of the ditch in the rear of his brigade's works, watching the show, when "a loud hurrahing was heard in our rear," and the bluecoats were seen pouring in on them from their left flank. At Jackson's command, Martin hurried to the left of the brigade with orders to move out by the right flank, and then hurried back to where he had left his general.

"Assisted by Lieutenant Colonel Gordon of my regiment," Martin continues, "the General was walking to where his horse had been sent; but the ground was thawing and the walking was slow and tedious. At every step our feet became encumbered with two or three pounds of stiff mud. The enemy were trying to cut us off and, though at some distance, were firing at us and calling out: 'Surrender!' The General was becoming exhausted, and requested the Colonel and myself to leave him. Being near the pike, Colonel Gordon told him that he thought we might get away. The General's horse was in the edge of the woods just beyond, and we felt we could reach the animal. I remained with the General, however.

"After crossing the pike and while getting over the stone fence, it rolled from under him and threw him into the ditch beyond. I assisted him out and persuaded him to pull his heavy boots off, as they were so loaded with mud that he could scarcely walk. He had got one off and was trying to remove the other when we heard the cry: 'Surrender, damn you!' Looking up, we saw the muzzles of four guns aimed at us across the fence, not more than seventy or eighty yards distant. 'They have got us, General,' I said, and called out: 'We surrender.'

"The General commenced to pull on his boot, and I turned his coat collar down to prevent our captors from discovering his rank, as I hoped we might be recaptured. The men—one corporal and three privates—sprang over the fence and came up to where we stood just as General Jackson succeeded in getting his boot on, and in pulling at it his collar assumed its natural position. The corporal walked around the General once or twice, then standing in front of him said: 'You are a General.' 'That is my rank,' was the reply. The corporal, taking off his hat, waved it around his head and cried out: 'Captured a General, by God! I will carry you to Nashville myself.'

"At a command in German from the corporal, two men took charge of the General and with the corporal crossed the fence to the pike and started with him toward the city, leaving me in charge of the other man, who in very strong language informed me that if I tried to run he would shoot my head off. I told him not to worry; I had run as far as I could. Then he started with me toward Nashville.

"We were on the edge of the ground over which Johnson's Division had fallen back, and blankets, knapsacks, etc., were scattered very liberally over it. The Dutchman told me to go to a very large knapsack, and when we reached it he proceeded to open and examine its contents. In kneeling to open it he let his gun fall into the hollow of his left arm, the muzzle almost touching my body. The temptation to knock him in the head took hold upon me; and while he was unbuckling the straps to the knapsack I jerked his gun and, whirling it, struck him back of the head. He fell across the knapsack, then I stepped over him and made off in the direction of the Franklin pike.

"Just as I entered the woods I met Lieutenant Colonel Gordon with General Jackson's horse. He asked me for General Jackson and I reported his capture. 'Mount his horse,' said the Colonel, 'We must get away from here, as the Yankee cavalry are trying to gain the pike in our rear.' We rode to the Franklin pike, where we saw demoralization in the extreme. Riding down the pike about a mile, we saw General Hood with other commanding officers trying to rally the men, but in vain. I saw one man who had been stopped by General Cheatham dodge beneath the General's horse and continue on his way while the General was trying to rally others."[40] Private Sam Watkins was not guilty of much exaggeration when he said that "it was like trying to stop the current of Duck River with a fish net."

As the routed forces of Cheatham's corps fled in disorder through the fields and over the hills in their rear toward the Franklin pike, the contagion of defeat spread rapidly down the Confederate line—and the equally contagious exhilaration of victory spread rapidly eastward along the Federal from Smith to Wood.

The victorious Federals sweeping eastward from their conquest of Shy's Hill swooped down on Stewart's exposed left flank so swiftly and unexpectedly that he had no time to improvise a defense. "Realizing their almost hopeless situation," recollects Major D. W. Sanders of French's division, "they abandoned their line and organizations and retreated in the wildest disorder and confusion. Many remained in the line and sur-

[40] *Confederate Veteran*, XVII, No. 1, p. 11.

rendered. In a few minutes the organizations of the corps on the left and center of the army had wholly disappeared, and the routed army rushed over the range of hills to the Franklin pike and filled it with a confused and ungovernable mass intent on escaping capture."[41]

But there were exceptions to this demoralization. Major Sanders records that "On the hillside facing east, in rear of the position held by Bate, was Major Truehart with a section of artillery, all that remained of his battalion, in command of his gunners, cool and deliberate, directing the fire of his guns into the advancing and victorious enemy, until he was surrounded and captured and his guns turned on the retreating Confederates. Truehart and his brave gunners, facing the enemy and intently serving his guns, his battalion colors flying while surrounded and captured, was the heroic figure on that historic field, so disastrous to Confederate arms."[42]

And Major Sanders also recalls that "On the range of hills south of the abandoned lines east from the Granny White pike was General Reynolds with his heroic brigade, intact in its organization, compact and soldierly on its last line, with Wilson's dismounted cavalrymen on the spur of the hills west of south from them. As they looked down upon their routed comrades, with many of whom they had fought side by side in the great battles of the Army of Tennessee from Shiloh to this fatal field, the spectacle was of a nature to have appalled even more heroic hearts."[43] Reynolds, however, was not appalled. Quickly comprehending the magnitude of the disaster, and operating in co-operation with Ector's brigade, Reynolds held the gap through which a country road crossed the hills in their rear until Cheatham's fleeing

41 *Southern Bivouac*, N.S., I, No. 3, p. 174.   42 *Ibid.*, 175.   43 *Ibid.*

men had passed through.[44] Then, and not until then, Reynolds and Coleman withdrew their brigades in order to the Franklin pike, in soldierly contrast to the panic of so many of their comrades.

The men in Lee's corps, on the Confederate right, were taken completely by surprise by the collapse and rout of their left and center. They had just successfully repulsed Wood's vigorous assault on their position and, says Lee, were "in fine spirits and confident of success." But within an hour, he goes on, "suddenly all eyes were turned to the center of our line of battle near the Granny White pike, where it was evident the enemy had made an entrance, although but little firing had been heard in that direction. Our men were flying to the rear in the wildest confusion, and the enemy following with enthusiastic cheers. The enemy at once closed toward the gap in our line and commenced charging on the left division (Johnson's) of my corps, but were handsomely driven back. The enemy soon gained our rear, and was moving on my left flank, when my line gradually gave way. My troops left their line in some disorder, but were soon rallied and presented a good front to the enemy."[45]

Lee's official report modestly omits any reference to his own zeal and gallantry manifested in attempting to turn the tide, but one of his men gives us a stirring picture of the heroic young commander in this fateful crisis:

"At the time of the break General Lee was sitting, mounted, in the rear of Clayton's division. Over on the left we could see confusion, and a Federal line advancing from the rear and attacking Johnson's division on

---

[44] This country road through the gap in the hills followed approximately the route of the present Overton Lea road and Lakeview Drive.

[45] *Official Records*, Vol. XLV, Pt. 1, 689.

the left wing of Lee's corps. Everything else had apparently been swept before it. Clayton's division was divided by the Franklin pike. General Lee rode across the pike, taking both stone fences, followed by one of his staff and two of his escort.

"He rode until he reached the rear of Stevenson's division of his corps, rode right into the midst of fugitives and in the face of the enemy who by this time had reached the rear of Pettus's brigade. General Lee seized a stand of colors from a color bearer and carried it on horse-back, appealing to the men to rally. 'Rally, men, rally! For God's sake, rally!' he cried. 'This is the place for brave men to die!' The effect was electrical. Men gathered in little knots of four or five, and he soon had around him three or four other stands of colors. The Federals, meeting this resistance, hesitated and halted. (It was late in the evening and misty.) The rally enabled Clayton's division to form a nucleus and establish a line of battle on one of the Overton Hills to the rear, crossing the Franklin pike in the woods near Colonel Overton's house. General Lee came back from his advanced position to this line. Here he was joined by a few pieces of artillery and a little drummer boy who beat the long roll in perfect time, as Gibson's brigade came up and formed a rear guard."[46]

It was a close thing. Only Lee's prompt action in rushing to the rear of Stevenson's division and rallying the men served to create the impression of organized resistance and caused the on-rushing Federals to halt their advance, at least temporarily. This gave Clayton and some of Stevenson's division time to fall to the rear in good order and form a new line. The Federals were advancing on the run and would surely have cut Clayton off, but for the Lee-inspired rally east of the pike.

[46] *Confederate Veteran,* XII, No. 7, p. 350.

The tidal wave of defeat descended so suddenly on
Lee's corps that there was not enough time to bring up
the artillery horses that had been sent to the rear, so
sixteen of Lee's guns were abandoned. He also lost large
numbers of prisoners as his men were engulfed and
surrounded by the advancing mass of Federals. Among
the prisoners was General Edward Johnson, who at first
approach of the attack from the west had formed his
men into a hollow square to receive the assault. But no
such drill-ground maneuver could long offset the pressure of superior numbers, and his hollow square quickly
melted away. Johnson had only recently been released
from a Federal prison, having been captured at the
battle of Spottsylvania Court House in May. Weakened
by his imprisonment and by a wound from which he
had not recovered, and being dismounted, he was easily
captured.

On the other side of the contending lines in this
closing action on the Confederate right, Wood relates
that after withdrawing and reposting the troops engaged
in the unsuccessful assault on Peach Orchard Hill, he
rode to his right to look to the condition of Kenner
Garrard's and Nathan Kimball's divisions. Shortly after
reaching his right, he says, "an electric shout, which announced that a grand advance was being made by our
right and right center, was borne from the right toward
the left. I at once ordered the whole corps to advance
and assault the enemy's works. . . . It rushed forward
like a mighty wave, driving everything before it"[47]—
but by this time there was really not much in Wood's
front to be driven.

Wood's report and the reports of his division commanders give the distinct impression that they carried

[47] *Official Records*, Vol. XLV, Pt. I, 134.

the Confederate position on Peach Orchard Hill by another brave charge in the face of great resistance, and there are some highly colored—and highly imaginative —prints showing such action taking place. "The Third Division reassaulted the Overton Hill, carrying it," Wood says in his report, and Beatty (the commander of the division) uses similar terms. In truth, however, Clayton had evacuated his works on the hill before Beatty's men got there, and the only men captured were the unresisting ones who stayed in the line, too tired or too discouraged to run. This fact is shown by the words used in the reports of Beatty's regimental commanders: "We again advanced in pursuit of enemy, who had been flanked from their works"; ". . . the enemy, having been routed on our right, fell back rapidly from their works in our front, and we advanced, pursuing them"; "We . . . saw the enemy leaving their works on the hill. The First Brigade was ordered forward, and our brigade followed them"; "The rebel works in our front were occupied with little or no resistance."[48]

Lee's corps, in the event of disaster, had been entrusted with the responsibility of holding the Franklin pike until the retreating Confederates could use it as an avenue of escape, and they performed this function in an eminently capable manner. As soon as it became obvious that the day was lost and that the only hope of the Confederates was to save what they could out of the wreckage of defeat, Lee moved to his appointed task with alacrity and efficiency.

Informed by Hood that the Federals were already near Brentwood, Lee quickly abandoned the line he had formed across the pike near the Overton house and hastened everything to the rear. A new rear guard line was

48 *Ibid.*, 134, 300, 303, 313, 317.

established at Hollow Tree Gap, beyond Brentwood and seven miles north of Franklin, at about 10 P.M. Wood's pursuit was not particularly energetic, and he bivouacked several miles short of Hollow Tree Gap when night fell.

Chalmers' cavalry had taken little effective part in the day's action until late in the afternoon. Morning had found him with Rucker's brigade where he had bivouacked on the Hillsboro pike at its intersection by the road to Brentwood. He was instructed to hold the pike, and this he did, skirmishing intermittently with detachments of Wilson's cavalry.

Late in the afternoon Chalmers, with his escort company and Forrest's "Old Regiment" under Colonel Kelley, moved across to the Granny White pike and held that pike until Cheatham's ambulances had withdrawn toward Franklin. In the unusual tactical situation at this stage of the battle, Chalmers was now in the rear of Wilson, who was in the rear of Cheatham, but Chalmers lacked enough men to make his position effective. A little later in the evening, Johnson's division of Wilson's cavalry had come across from the Charlotte pike and attacked Rucker on the Hillsboro pike. Rucker was then withdrawn to the Granny White pike, uniting with Kelley's regiment, and the whole brigade (with the exception of the Seventh Tennessee, which had been sent down the Hillsboro pike to Franklin) formed in front of Brentwood to protect the wagons and ambulances collected there.

About 4:30 P.M. Chalmers received Hood's frantic message to "hold the Granny White pike at all hazards." The brigade was accordingly moved onto that pike and took a position across it just north of the road to Brentwood, constructing a stout barricade of logs, brush and fence rails. Soon the victorious and elated troopers of

Hatch, Hammond, and Croxton, now back in the saddle, came plunging out the pike, through the gathering darkness and the downpour of rain that was freezing as it fell.

Only temporarily disconcerted by the unexpected obstacle in their path, the blue-coated riders formed front into line and charged the barricade, thousands against hundreds. At the time of the onslaught Colonel Rucker was about a half mile in the rear, where he had gone to find a position for a section of artillery, leaving to Colonel Kelley the immediate command of the troops behind the barricade. Although overwhelmingly outnumbered, Kelley and his men held on tenaciously, and what General Wilson described as "one of the fiercest conflicts that ever took place in the Civil War" ensued. Although the outcome of such an unequal struggle could never be in doubt, this remnant of Forrest's cavalry fought with uncommon fierceness and held Wilson's men in check while the retreating infantry were passing Brentwood on the Franklin pike.

The battle at the barricade, and in the adjoining fields to which it overflowed, finally degenerated into a veritable dog-fight of hand-to-hand individual combat. In the pitch-black darkness it was almost impossible to distinguish friend from foe, as the battle line surged backward and forward. Colonel Rucker was soon involved in the fray, and a dramatic episode ensued when he encountered a mounted opponent who, in the darkness, identified himself as Colonel George Spalding of the Twelfth Tennessee (Federal) Cavalry. Rucker grabbed Spalding's bridle rein, crying out: "You are my prisoner, for I am Colonel Ed Rucker of the Twelfth Tennessee Rebel Cavalry." Spalding replied defiantly, "Not by a damned sight!" and, spurring his horse, broke loose from Rucker's grasp. At this juncture, Captain

Joseph C. Boyer of Spalding's regiment joined in the fracas and wrenched Rucker's saber from his hand—but, in an almost incredible twist of events, Rucker in turn possessed himself of Boyer's saber. In the pelting rain, their hands benumbed by the cold, the two riders engaged in a grim duel in the darkness. The fight was ended when a pistol shot from another Federal trooper broke Rucker's sword arm (which was later amputated in a Nashville hospital) and compelled his surrender.

Wilson writes with colorful enthusiasm of this wild night fight there on the Granny White pike: "It was a scene of pandemonium," he says, "in which flashing carbines, whistling bullets, bursting shells and the imprecations of struggling men filled the air. . . . Every officer and man did his full duty in the headlong rush which finally drove Chalmers and his gallant horsemen from the field, in hopeless rout and confusion. They had stood their ground bravely, but were overborne at every turn and at every stand by the weight and fury of the Union onset."[49]

Chalmers's last stand had been a desperate and costly one, but it had accomplished its purpose. What was left of the brigade withdrew unpursued to the Franklin pike, and when the last of the retreating infantry and artillery had passed, the weary troopers camped on the pike for the night with the rear guard. Wilson, his men badly scattered and tired out with a full day's fighting, gave orders just before midnight for each command to bivouac where orders overtook it, and to take up the pursuit the next morning.

As he was riding down the Granny White pike after giving these orders, Wilson was overtaken by General Thomas, who pulled up abreast of him in the darkness and called out "Is that you, Wilson?" Answered in the

[49] Wilson, *Under the Old Flag*, II, 124.

affirmative, Thomas exclaimed in a voice "that might have been heard a quarter of a mile": "Dang it to hell, Wilson, didn't I tell you we could lick 'em?" Thomas was a mild-mannered man, not given to the use of strong language, but Wilson says that he ripped out that "dang it" "with all the vehemence of an old dragoon," and then galloped back toward Nashville.

A mile or so away on the Franklin pike the commander of the other, the defeated, army, was sitting disconsolate in his tent by the side of the road. Private Sam Watkins, who had been wounded in the engagement, had had his wounds bandaged and then boldly sought out General Hood to ask for "a wounded furlough." He has left an unforgettable picture of his commander as he found him in his tent: "He was much agitated and affected, pulling his hair with one hand (he had but one) and crying like his heart would break."[50] Hood readily gave the wounded private the scrap of paper he sought, and Watkins went back out into the rain and joined the bedraggled survivors of the dreadful two days of fighting as they slogged down the muddy road.

Somewhere along the line some irrepressible wag, with the indestructible *élan* of the Army of Tennessee, had improvised a parody of the popular song "The Yellow Rose of Texas," and he and his sodden, bloody comrades were singing:

> So now we're going to leave you, our hearts are full of woe;
> We're going back to Georgia to see our Uncle Joe.
> You may talk about your Beauregard and sing of General Lee,
> But the gallant Hood of Texas played hell in Tennessee.

50 Sam R. Watkins, *"Co. Aytch"* (Nashville, 1882), 229.

Epilogue

THE next ten days were a nightmare of nerve-wracking hardship and struggle to both armies. Alternately marching and fighting, worn down by battle fatigue and sheer physical exhaustion, they somehow managed to carry on an almost continuous running battle from Nashville to the Tennessee River. The weather was abominable—rain, sleet and snow, with below-freezing temperatures. The wagons and guns quickly churned the roads into seemingly bottomless quagmires, which froze into sharp-edged ruts during the cold nights. The heavy rains not only drenched the suffering soldiers but soon flooded the streams and made the passage of each of them a serious problem.

Hood's defeat-shocked army was on short rations—mostly parched corn, with an occasional feast of corn pone and fat bacon or perhaps a pilfered pig or pullet. A fortunate few had blankets or overcoats picked up on the battlefield, but most of them had only their threadbare uniforms to protect them from the icy rain that seemed to pierce to the very marrow of their bones. Many had no hats to cover their heads; but it was the scarcity of shoes that presented an especially acute problem. The number of men who were wholly or partially barefooted is almost unbelievable, and Hood's weary veterans literally left bloody footprints in the roads as they stumbled over the frozen ruts. Major James D. Porter, of Cheatham's staff, relates that at one point on the retreat, when the tired and underfed horses were unable to pull a wagon train up a steep hill covered with ice, Cheatham ordered him to get a hundred well-shod men from the ranks to help push the wagons up the hill. After diligent search, Porter says, he was able to find in the whole corps a total of twenty-five men who had whole shoes on their feet.[1]

Thomas' men had no such trouble as this. They were well shod, well clothed, and well fed, but they had their share of difficulties. And a steady downpour of freezing rain, with muddy roads and swollen streams, will slow down the progress of the most excellently equipped army. The higher-ups in their Washington armchairs, however, did not seem to appreciate this fact, and they were soon back at their seemingly favorite pastime: nagging a commander in the field to show greater activity.

General Thomas on the evening of December 16 had sent a telegram to President Lincoln, Secretary Stanton, General Grant, and Governor Andrew Johnson of Tennessee, giving them a detailed report of his crushing victory over Hood. Perhaps in an effort to head off any suggestions, he concluded his report with the statement, "I have ordered the pursuit to be continued in the morning at daylight, although the troops are very much fatigued."[2]

The immediate reaction to the news of the battle's outcome was one of joy and exultation throughout the Union. One of the first to congratulate Thomas was Admiral Lee, in command of the gunboats on the river. He praised Thomas for "the signal defeat of General Hood's army, in which centered the strength and hopes of half the rebellion," expressing the belief that the con-

[1] Interview with Porter in Nashville *Banner* (undated clipping in author's possession).
[2] *Official Records*, Vol. XLV, Pt. II, 210.

sequences of the battle would be "more important than have followed the previous achievements of the war." Secretary Stanton sent a telegram to each of the governors of the Northern states, and to the commanders of the other Union armies, informing them of the "great and decisive victory" of Thomas over Hood.[3]

General Meade, from his headquarters before Petersburg, sent a telegram to Stanton, saying: "I congratulate the President, yourself, and the country on the glorious victory achieved by Major-General Thomas and the troops under his command. I have directed a salute of 100 guns to be fired to-morrow at sunrise in honor of this brilliant triumph." It apparently did not occur to Meade to send any congratulations to the man who had achieved the brilliant triumph, but nobody seemed to notice that. Little Phil Sheridan, from his headquarters in the Shenandoah Valley, sent a congratulatory telegram to Thomas referring to his "brilliant victory" and concluding: "We have given you 200 guns and much cheering."[4]

Grant was in no hurry about sending congratulations, but did telegraph Thomas on December 18, stating that the armies operating against Richmond "have fired 200 guns in honor of your great victory." Governor Johnson sent him a message of praise for "the great victory" he had won, stating that "its withering influence upon rebels is more decided than anything which has transpired since the beginning of the rebellion."[5]

Thomas had moved out promptly with his pursuing army on December 17, and on December 18 from near Spring Hill telegraphed Halleck that he had that day captured "the rebel Brigadier-General Quarles," who had been wounded at the battle of Franklin and was

[3] *Ibid.,* 227, 230.   [4] *Ibid.,* 230.   [5] *Ibid.,* 248, 471.

hospitalized in a nearby house. He was careful to point out that the enemy was being "vigorously pursued" and that the pursuit would be continued the next day.[6]

On December 19 Thomas reported to Halleck that the infantry had not been able to move that day, owing to heavy rains which had made the streams impassable. But there were no heavy rains or impassable streams in the Washington offices, and Halleck on December 21 resumed his schoolteacherish attitude to Thomas, telegraphing him: "Permit me, general, to urge the vast importance of a hot pursuit. . . . If you can capture or destroy Hood's army Sherman can entirely crush out the rebel military force in all the Southern States. . . . A most vigorous pursuit on your part is therefore of vital importance. . . ."[7]

Thomas, at long last tired of turning the other cheek, replied with an unwonted show of spirit: "General Hood's army is being pursued as rapidly and as vigorously as it is possible for one army to pursue another. We cannot control the elements. . . . pursuing an enemy through an exhausted country, over mud roads, completely sogged with heavy rains, is no child's play. . . ."[8]

Secretary Stanton, when he saw this exchange of messages, quickly telegraphed Thomas in fulsome terms: "It is proper for me to assure you that this Department has the most unbounded confidence in your skill, vigor, and determination to employ to the best advantage all the means in your power to pursue and destroy the enemy. No Department could be inspired with more profound admiration and thankfulness for the great deeds you have already performed, or more confiding faith that human effort could accomplish no more than will be done by you and the gallant officers and soldiers of your command."[9]

6 *Ibid.*, 249-50.   7 *Ibid.*, 265, 295.   8 *Ibid.*, 295-96.   9 *Ibid.*, 307.

Even Grant softened sufficiently to telegraph Thomas on December 22: "You have the congratulations of the public for the energy with which you are pushing Hood"—but he could not refrain from adding: "If you succeed in destroying Hood's army there will be but one army left to the so-called Confedracy capable of doing us harm. I will take care of that and try to draw the sting from it. . . ."[10] Thomas was probably surprised and pleased at the mellow tone of this message, but he would not have been so pleased if he could have known that within a few days Grant would be writing to Sherman, complaining querulously of Thomas' "sluggishness."

"With the exception of the rear guard, [Hood's] army had become a disheartened and disorganized rabble of half-armed and barefooted men . . . ," Thomas wrote in his official report. He was generous and truthful enough, however, to add: "The rear guard . . . was undaunted and firm, and did its work bravely to the last"[11]—a handsome and well-deserved tribute from an admiring adversary.

In the nature of things, any opinion General Thomas may have had as to the morale of Hood's defeated army could not have been founded on anything more substantial than hearsay. Major James D. Porter, who participated in the retreat, gives a first-hand account of it which does not substantiate the exaggerated expressions used in Thomas's report.

"Immediately after the break in our line," Porter says, "the troops sought their own organizations, reformed under their officers, and marched out of the state in perfect order. . . . The men, with occasional exceptions, had arms in their hands. At Franklin there were

10 *Ibid.* Van Horne, *Life of Thomas*, 361.   11 *Ibid.*, Pt. I, 42.

General John Bell Hood, C.S.A.

Major General George Henry Thomas, U.S.A.

Stockade and parapet of Capitol fortifications, from east side looking southeast (*Library of Congress*); Stockade and guns on east side
of Capitol looking north (*Library of Congress*).

Railroad bridge at Nashville during Federal occupation, planked
over for vehicular traffic and equipped with sentry boxes

Library of Congress

The stockaded State Capitol, with soldiers' tents and "bush arbors" in foreground (*Library of Congress*); View of portico of stockaded Capitol, looking north (*Library of Congress*).

View of Thomas' outer line just after Smith's corps had advanced.
Campfires are still smouldering to the right, with the wagons in the
background (*Library of Congress*); Thomas' inner defensive line
during the battle (*Library of Congress*).

Spectators (civilians and soldiers not taking part in the action) watch
the battle on December 15 (*Library of Congress*); Watching the
battle from the Military College (*Library of Congress*).

One of the casements of Fort Negley, armored with railroad iron. Confederate center and left on hills in distance (*Library of Congress*); Charge of Minnesota troops, December 16, 1864 (*From a painting by Howard Pyle, Courtesy Minnesota Historical Society*).

several thousand stand of arms, a very large proportion captured from the enemy; and after the loss of fifty pieces of artillery, the army retired with fifty-nine field pieces and an ample supply of ammunition. The successful resistance to the assault of the Federal cavalry near Franklin by the rear guard of Lee's corps, repeated the next day by the rear guard of Cheatham's corps, does not sustain the Federal general's report that our army was a 'disorganized rabble.' "[12]

Thomas' characterization of Hood's surviving troops as "a disheartened and disorganized rabble," a characterization which has been accepted and repeated by subsequent writers of history, indicates that he was somehow betrayed into using stronger terms than were justified by the facts. He was on firm ground, however, in what he said about the spirit of the rear guard. Hood's rear guard during those trying days was indeed undaunted and firm, and deserving of every possible word of praise for a prodigious performance under the greatest difficulties.

The main body of Hood's army, following the collapse on the evening of December 16, was pretty thoroughly whipped and dispirited. The survivors of Cheatham's and Stewart's corps, after their flight from the battlefield, had proceeded precipitately down the Franklin pike, with orders to push on to Franklin that night and to Spring Hill the next day. Lee, with two brigades of infantry, held the pike at Hollow Tree Gap. Buford's cavalry brigade, having been notified of Hood's defeat, made a forced march across country during the night to join with Chalmers in helping Lee defend the pike, the Confederates' sole line of retreat. All they could hope to do, however, was slow down the pursuit, and they all

[12] General Clement A. Evans (ed.), *Confederate Military History*, 12 vols. (Atlanta, 1899), X, 168.

fell back in the direction of Franklin the next morning when assailed by Wilson's hard-driving cavalry in front and on the flanks.

Lee and the rear guard did not tarry long when they got to Franklin, but burned the bridge and moved on southward the next morning, closely followed by the pursuing Federals, who were able to cross the Harpeth without much delay. Early in the afternoon there was a spirited skirmish about two miles south of Franklin, about where the Confederate army had formed for the attack on November 30. In the course of this affair Lee was wounded, but continued to lead the rear guard until nightfall, when he was forced to turn over the command of the corps to Stevenson. Late in the afternoon there was another engagement between the pursuers and the pursued in a large beech grove four miles north of Spring Hill, of which Lee says: "A more persistent effort was never made to rout the rear guard of a retiring column."[13] The rear guard refused to be routed, however; on the contrary it sharply repulsed the attacking Federals, and then withdrew in order and camped for the night.

On December 18 Cheatham's corps replaced Lee's in the rear guard, and the cavalry was strengthened by the addition of the brigade of General Armstrong, who overtook them that morning. The rear guard moved on down the pike from Spring Hill, stopping occasionally for some skirmishing during the day. On the evening of December 19, after another day of fire-and-fall-back encounters with the bluecoats, the last of the Confederates crossed to the south side of Duck River at Columbia, where Forrest had just arrived from Murfreesboro.

Forrest on the evening of December 15 had been reached by a courier with a message from Hood inform-

13 *Official Records*, Vol. XLV, Pt. I, 690.

ing him that a general engagement was in progress at Nashville and ordering him to hold himself in readiness to move at any moment. In compliance, Forrest next morning assembled his entire command at Wilkinson Cross Roads, six miles from Murfreesboro on the Wilkinson pike. When that night he received the news of the rout of Hood's army, he immediately sent Buford to help protect Hood's retreat, while he moved in the direction of Duck River to rejoin the retreating army. The infantry under his command, he says in his report, were mostly barefooted, and he was encumbered with several hundred head of hogs and cattle, so he could move but slowly. Forrest was a master of forced marches, however, and he had his whole command in Columbia by the afternoon of December 19, ready to assume the responsibility of protecting the rear of the retreat.

Hood had originally intended to make a stand when he got across Duck River, but when he saw the shattered condition of his army he quickly realized the futility of that. Accordingly he moved on from Columbia with the main body of his troops on the morning of December 20, but before leaving he formally assigned the command of the rear guard to Forrest, with instructions to hold the town as long as he could and then follow Hood through Pulaski in the direction of Florence, Alabama. Forrest immediately pointed out the necessity for a greater infantry force in the rear guard if any effective defensive action was to be maintained, and at his suggestion General Walthall was put in command of eight picked brigades, a forlorn little elite corps, to serve under Forrest. To Walthall's own three brigades, five others were added, and they were temporarily reorganized and consolidated into four brigade outfits: Featherston's and Quarles's under command of General Featherston; Ector's and Reynolds' under General Reynolds;

Strahl's and Maney's under Colonel Feild; and Smith's and Palmer's under Colonel J. B. Palmer.

The decimated condition of Hood's army is strikingly evidenced by the fact that these eight brigades, nominally embracing more than thirty regiments, mustered only 1,920 effectives: Palmer, 616; Featherston, 498; Feild, 278; and Reynolds, 528—less than 2,000 men with guns in their hands, and 400 of these barefooted.[14] The resourceful Forrest, however, quickly worked out a practical (if unmilitary) solution for this difficulty: the barefooted men were permitted to ride in the wagons while the force was on the march; then, when there was fighting to do, they jumped down from the wagons, resumed their places in the ranks and fought on foot— barefoot.

Forrest was given a little breathing spell in which to organize his makeshift command into workable condition. The heavy rains had resulted in a freshet in Duck River that made it unfordable, so it was not until December 22 that the Federals were able to cross the river on a hastily constructed pontoon bridge and resume the pursuit. Forrest had ordered Walthall and his infantry to retire down the main pike from Columbia to Pulaski while the cavalry covered the rear on both flanks of the pike, with a picket line across the road at Warfield's three miles south of Columbia.

The advancing Federals opened on this picket line with artillery when they got there, whereupon Forrest fell back to a point where the road passed through a narrow gap, and there the Federal advance was checked. On the night of December 23 he halted his command at Lynnville and the next morning ordered the infantry to march back from Pulaski and join him. They then turned and advanced on the pursuing Federals in an

14 *Ibid.*, 728-30; 757.

audacious surprise attack, and a brisk engagement ensued. Forrest then fell back to Richland Creek, where there was another spirited skirmish in which General Buford was wounded and disabled. Attrition was getting in its deadly work on the rear guard—and the Federals kept on coming.

On a cold Christmas morning the advanced ranks of Hood's infantry reached the Tennessee River at Bainbridge, a few miles above Florence. Here a pontoon bridge was speedily constructed, on which the army began crossing the river the next morning, and then began the long march to Tupelo, Mississippi, their designated destination. Forrest and the rear guard made a stand at Pulaski on Christmas Day, and on the twenty-sixth maneuvered their pursuers into a sort of ambush which, Forrest says, resulted in their "complete rout," and the capture of one piece of Federal artillery. His report continues: "The enemy was pursued for two miles, but showing no disposition to give battle my troops were ordered back." [15]

That was about the last real effort by the Federals to impede the Confederate retreat. The gunboats on the river shelled the pontoon bridge but were soon driven off by Hood's artillery. Forrest and the last of the rear guard crossed the Tennessee on December 27, and on the twenty-ninth Thomas issued General Orders declaring the pursuit at an end.

Describing the campaign as "brilliant in its achievements and unsurpassed in its results by any other of this war," the General Orders closed in a burst of turgid rhetoric which was entirely uncharacteristic of Thomas and which must constitute one of the longest single sentences ever written:

"That veteran rebel army which, though driven from

15 *Ibid.,* 758.

position to position, opposed a stubborn resistance to much superior numbers during the whole of the Atlanta campaign, taking advantage of the absence of the largest portion of the army which had been opposed to it in Georgia, invaded Tennessee, buoyant with hope, expecting Nashville, Murfreesborough and the whole of Tennessee and Kentucky to fall into its power an easy prey, and scarcely fixing a limit to its conquests, after having received the most terrible check at Franklin, on the 30th of November, that any army has received during this war, and later met with a signal repulse from the brave garrison at Murfreesborough in its attempt to capture that place, was finally attacked at Nashville, and although your forces were inferior to it in numbers, it was hurled back from the coveted prize upon which it had only been permitted to look from a distance, and finally sent flying, dismayed and disordered, whence it came, impelled by the instinct of self-preservation, and thinking only how it could relieve itself for short intervals from your persistent and harassing pursuit, by burning the bridges over the swollen streams as it passed them, until finally it had placed the broad waters of the Tennessee River between you and its shattered, diminished, and discomfited columns, leaving its artillery and battle-flags in your victorious hands, lasting trophies of your noble daring and lasting mementoes of the enemy's disgrace and defeat." Thomas placed his official casualties for the two days' battle at 3,061.[16]

Thomas, of course, was sadly misinformed if he really thought the "veteran rebel army" had superior numbers either in the Atlanta campaign or in the battle of Nashville. He was on safe ground in referring to that army's "defeat" at Nashville. There was no question about

[16] *Ibid.*, 50, 105.

that. But the use of the word "disgrace" seems out of place. General Schofield certainly did not feel that the defeated army was disgraced. On the contrary, he was frank enough to say that their loss of the battle was not due to any lack of valor but to their inferior numbers. Recalling a conversation with a captured Confederate officer, he says: "In answer to my question as to when the Confederate troops recognized the fact that they were beaten, he answered, 'Not till you routed us just now.' . . . I doubt if any soldiers in the world ever needed so much cumulative evidence to convince them that they were beaten."[17]

Hood's official report of the battle of Nashville to General Beauregard, written January 9 at Tupelo, is a masterpiece of half-truths, imparting the news of a disaster in carefully sugar-coated terms:

"Nothing of importance occurred till the morning of the 15th of December, when the enemy attacked simultaneously both our flanks. On our right he was handsomely repulsed, with heavy loss, but on our left he succeeded in driving in our flank, and toward evening carried some partially completed works which were in process of erection for the protection of this flank. Our line being necessarily very extended, a series of works had been commenced on each flank for their protection. During the night of the 15th our whole line was shortened and our left thrown back, and dispositions were made to meet any renewed attack. . . .

"Early on the 16th of December the enemy made a general attack on our lines, accompanied by a very heavy fire of artillery. All his assaults were repulsed with great loss till 3:30 p.m., when a portion of our line to the left of the center, occupied by Bate's division, suddenly gave way. In a few minutes our entire line was

17 Schofield, *Forty-six Years in the Army*, 248.

broken, our troops retreating rapidly down the pike in the direction of Franklin, most of them, I regret to say, in great confusion, and all efforts to reform them were fruitless. Our loss in artillery was heavy, the giving way of the lines being so sudden that it was impossible to bring away the guns that had been placed in position. Our loss in killed and wounded was small."[18] Hood stated that his total loss in the entire Tennessee campaign did not exceed 10,000—but this was probably an underestimate.

Sugar-coat it as much as he chose, however, Hood in his heart knew the bitter truth. His invasion of Tennessee, the last flare-up of aggressive military action by the Southern Confederacy, had ended in disastrous failure. His vision of a victorious Confederate army advancing to the Ohio River was to remain a dream. The Confederate battle flags would not be seen waving in Cincinnati or Chicago, a possibility Grant had pictured. The battle of Nashville had decided that—and thereby decided the fate of the Confederate States of America.

It was at Nashville that Hood, wisely or not, risked all on one cast of the military dice, and lost. For it was by the battle of Nashville, as one of Thomas' biographers has so well said, that "one of the two great armies of the Confederacy was eliminated from the final problem, and with the total overthrow of that army, the very cause which it had so long and so gallantly sustained was lost."[19]

18 *Official Records,* Vol. XLV, Pt. I, 660.
19 Hood, *Advance and Retreat,* 310; Van Horne, *Life of Thomas,* 336.

Organization of the Federal Forces

Commanded by Major General George H. Thomas

December 15, 1864

INFANTRY

FOURTH ARMY CORPS, Brig. Gen. Thomas J. Wood

First Division, Brig. Gen. Nathan Kimball

First Brigade, Col. Isaac M. Kirby—21st Illinois, Capt. William H. Jamison; 38th Illinois, Capt. Andrew M. Pollard; 31st Indiana, Col. John T. Smith; 81st Indiana, Maj. Edward C. Mathey; 90th Ohio, Lieut. Col. Samuel N. Yeoman; 101st Ohio, Lieut. Col. Bedan B. McDonald.

Second Brigade, Brig. Gen. Walter C. Whitaker—96th Illinois, Maj. George Hicks; 115th Illinois, Col. Jesse H. Moore; 35th Indiana, Lieut. Col. Augustus C. Tassin; 21st Kentucky, Lieut. Col. James C. Evans; 23rd Kentucky, Lieut. Col. George W. Northup; 45th Ohio, Lieut. Col. John H. Humphrey; 51st Ohio, Lieut. Col. Charles H. Wood.

Third Brigade, Brig. Gen. William Grose—75th Illinois, Col. John E. Bennett; 80th Illinois, Capt. James Cunningham; 84th Illinois, Lieut. Col. Charles H. Morton; 9th Indiana, Col. Isaac C. B. Suman; 30th Indiana, Capt. Henry W. Lawton; 36th Indiana (one company), Lieut. Col. John P. Swisher; 84th Indiana, Maj. John C. Taylor; 77th Pennsylvania, Col. Thomas E. Rose.

Second Division, Brig. Gen. Washington L. Elliott

First Brigade, Col. Emerson Opdycke—36th Illinois, Maj. Levi P. Holden; 44th Illinois, Capt. Alonzo W. Clark; 73rd Illinois, Capt. Wilson Burroughs; 74th and 88th Illinois, Lieut. Col. George W. Smith; 125th Ohio, Maj. Joseph Bruff; 24th Wisconsin, Capt. William Kennedy.

Second Brigade, Col. John Q. Lane—100th Illinois, Lieut. Col. Charles M. Hammond; 40th Indiana, Lieut. Col. Henry Leaming; 57th Indiana, Lieut. Col. Willis Blanch; 28th Kentucky, Maj. George W. Barth, Lieut. Col. J. Rowan Boone; 26th Ohio, Capt. William Clark; 97th Ohio, Lieut. Col. Milton Barnes.

Third Brigade, Col. Joseph Conrad—42nd Illinois, Lieut. Col. Edgar D. Swain; 51st Illinois, Capt. Albert M. Tilton; 79th Illinois (with veteran detachment 27th Illinois attached), Col. Allen Buckner; 15th Missouri, Capt. George Ernst; 64th Ohio, Lieut. Col. Robert C. Brown; 65th Ohio, Maj. Orlow Smith.

Third Division; Brig. Gen. Samuel Beatty

First Brigade, Col. Abel D. Streight—89th Illinois, Lieut. Col. William D. Williams; 51st Indiana, Capt. William W. Scearce; 8th Kansas, Lieut. Col. John Conover; 15th Ohio, Col. Frank Askew; 49th Ohio, Maj. Luther M. Strong.

Second Brigade, Col. P. Sidney Post—59th Illinois, Maj. James M. Stookey; 41st Ohio, Lieut. Col. Robert L. Kimberly; 71st Ohio, Lieut. Col. James H. Hart; 93rd Ohio, Lieut. Col. Daniel Bowman; 124th Ohio, Lieut. Col. James Pickands.

Third Brigade, Col. Frederick Knefler—79th Indiana, Lieut. Col. George W. Parker; 86th Indiana, Col. George F. Dick; 13th Ohio (four companies), Maj. Joseph T. Snider; 19th Ohio, Col. Henry G. Stratton.

Artillery, Maj. Wilbur F. Goodspeed—Indiana Light 25th Battery, Capt. Frederick C. Sturm; Kentucky Light, 1st Battery, Capt. Theodore S. Thomasson; 1st Michigan Light, Battery E, Capt. Peter De Vries; 1st Ohio Light, Battery G, Capt. Alexander Marshall; Ohio Light, 6th Battery, Lieut. Aaron P. Baldwin; Pennsylvania Light, Battery B, Capt. Jacob Ziegler; 4th United States, Battery M, Lieut. Samuel Canby.

TWENTY-THIRD ARMY CORPS, Maj. Gen. John M. Schofield

Second Division, Maj. Gen. Darius N. Couch

First Brigade, Brig. Gen. Joseph A. Cooper—130th Indiana, Col. Charles S. Parrish; 26th Kentucky, Col. Cicero Maxwell; 25th Michigan, Capt. Samuel L. Demarest; 99th Ohio, Lieut. Col. John E. Cummins; 3rd Tennessee, Col. William Cross; 6th Tennessee, Lieut. Col. Edward Maynard.

Second Brigade, Col. Orlando H. Moore—107th Illinois, Capt. John W. Wood; 80th Indiana, Lieut. Col. Alfred D. Owen; 129th Indiana, Col. Charles A. Zollinger; 23rd Michigan, Col. Oliver L. Spaulding; 111th Ohio, Lieut. Col. Isaac R. Sherwood; 118th Ohio, Maj. Edgar Sowers.

Third Brigade, Col. John Mehringer—91st Indiana, Lieut. Col. Charles H. Butterfield; 123rd Indiana, Col. John C. McQuiston; 50th Ohio, Lieut. Col. Hamilton S. Gillespie; 183rd Ohio, Col. George W. Hoge.

Artillery—Indiana Light, 15th Battery, Capt. Alonzo D. Harvey; Ohio Light, 19th Battery, Capt. Frank Wilson.

Third Division, Brig. Gen. Jacob D. Cox

First Brigade, Col. Charles C. Doolittle—12th Kentucky, Lieut. Col. Laurence H. Rousseau; 16th Ken-

tucky, Capt. Jacob Miller; 100th Ohio, Lieut Col.
Edwin L. Hayes; 104th Ohio, Col. Oscar W. Sterl; 8th
Tennessee, Capt. James W. Berry.

Second Brigade, Col. John S. Casement—65th Illinois, Lieut. Col. W. Scott Stewart; 65th Indiana, Lieut.
Col. John W. Hammond; 124th Indiana, Col. John M.
Orr; 103rd Ohio, Capt. Henry S. Pickands; 5th Tennessee, Lieut. Col. Nathaniel Witt.

Third Brigade, Col. Israel N. Stiles—112th Illinois,
Maj. Tristram T. Dow; 63rd Indiana, Lieut. Col.
Daniel Morris; 120th Indiana, Maj. John M. Barcus;
128th Indiana, Lieut. Col. Jasper Packard.

Artillery—Indiana Light, 23rd Battery, Lieut. Aaron
A. Wilbur; 1st Ohio Light, Battery D, Capt. Giles J.
Cockerill.

DETACHMENT ARMY OF THE TENNESSEE (Six-teenth Army Corps), Maj. Gen. Andrew J. Smith

First Division, Brig. Gen. John McArthur

First Brigade, Col. William L. McMillen—114th Il-
linois, Capt. John M. Johnson; 93rd Indiana, Col. De-
Witt C. Thomas; 10th Minnesota, Lieut. Col. Samuel
P. Jennison; 72nd Ohio, Lieut. Col. Charles G. Eaton;
95th Ohio, Lieut. Col. Jefferson Brumback; Illinois
Light Artillery, Cogswell's Battery, Lieut. S. Hamilton
McClaury.

Second Brigade, Col. Lucius F. Hubbard—5th Min-
nesota, Lieut. Col. William B. Gere; 9th Minnesota,
Col. Josiah F. Marsh; 11th Missouri, Lieut. Col. Eli
Bowyer; 8th Wisconsin, Lieut. Col. William B. Britton;
Iowa Light Artillery, 2nd Battery, Capt. Joseph R.
Reed.

Third Brigade, Col. Sylvester G. Hill—12th Iowa,
Lieut. Col. John H. Stibbs; 35th Iowa, Maj. William

Dill; 7th Minnesota, Col. William R. Marshall; 33rd Missouri, Lieut. Col. William H. Heath; 2nd Missouri Light Artillery, Battery I, Capt. Stephen H. Julian.

Second Division, Brig. Gen. Kenner Garrard

First Brigade, Col. David Moore—119th Illinois, Col. Thomas J. Kinney; 122nd Illinois, Lieut. Col. James F. Drish; 89th Indiana, Lieut. Col. Hervey Craven; 21st Missouri (detachment of 24th Missouri attached), Lieut. Col. Edwin Moore; Indiana Light Artillery, 9th Battery, Lieut. Samuel G. Calfee.

Second Brigade, Col. James I. Gilbert—58th Illinois, Maj. Robert W. Healy; 27th Iowa, Lieut. Col. Jed Lake; 32nd Iowa, Lieut. Col. Gustavus A. Eberhart; 10th Kansas (four companies), Capt. William C. Jones; Indiana Light Artillery, 3rd Battery, Lieut. Thomas J. Ginn.

Third Brigade, Col. Edward H. Wolfe—49th Illinois, Col. Phineas Pease; 117th Illinois, Col. Jonathan Merriam; 52nd Indiana, Lieut. Col. Zalmon S. Main; 178th New York, Capt. John B. Gandolfo; 2nd Illinois Light Artillery, Battery G, Capt. John W. Lowell (Chief of division artillery).

Third Division, Col. Jonathan B. Moore

First Brigade, Col. Lyman M. Ward—72nd Illinois, Capt. James A. Sexton; 40th Missouri, Col. Samuel A. Holmes; 14th Wisconsin, Maj. Eddy F. Ferris; 33rd Wisconsin, Lieut. Col. Frederick S. Lovell.

Second Brigade, Col. Leander Blanden—81st Illinois, Lieut. Col. Andrew W. Rogers; 95th Illinois, Lieut. Col. William Avery; 44th Missouri, Lieut. Col. Andrew J. Barr.

Artillery—Indiana Light, 14th Battery, Capt. Francis W. Morse; 2nd Missouri Light, Battery A, Lieut. John Zepp.

PROVISIONAL DETACHMENT (DISTRICT OF THE ETOWAH), Maj. Gen. James B. Steedman

Provisional Division, Brig. Gen. Charles Cruft

First Brigade, Col. Benjamin Harrison.

Second Brigade, Col. John G. Mitchell.

Third Brigade, Col. Charles H. Grosvenor.

Miscellaneous—68th Indiana (attached to Third Brigade) Lieut. Col. Harvey J. Espy; 18th Ohio (attached to Third Brigade), Capt. Ebenezer Grosvenor.

Artillery—Indiana Light, 20th Battery, Capt. Milton A. Osborne; Ohio Light, 18th Battery, Capt. Charles C. Aleshire.

First Colored Brigade, Col. Thomas J. Morgan—14th U. S. Colored Troops, Lieut. Col. Henry C. Corbin; 16th U.S.C.T. (detached with pontoon train) Col. William B. Gaw; 17th U.S.C.T., Col. William R. Shafter; 18th U.S.C.T. (battalion), Maj. Lewis D. Joy; 44th U.S.C.T., Col. Lewis Johnson.

Second Colored Brigade, Col. Charles R. Thompson —12th U.S. Colored Troops, Lieut. Col. William R. Sellon; 13th U.S.C.T., Col. John A. Hottenstein; 100th U.S.C.T., Maj. Collin Ford; Kansas Light Artillery, 1st Battery, Capt. Marcus D. Tenney.

POST OF NASHVILLE, Brig. Gen. John F. Miller

Second Brigade, Fourth Division, Twentieth Army Corps, Col. Edward C. Mason—142nd Indiana, Col. John M. Comparet; 45th New York, Lieut. Col. Adolphus Dobke; 176th Ohio, Lieut. Col. William B. Nesbitt; 179th Ohio, Col. Harley H. Sage; 182nd Ohio, Col. Lewis Butler.

Unattached—3rd Kentucky; 28th Michigan, Col. William W. Wheeler; 173rd Ohio, Col. John R. Hurd; 78th Pennsylvania (detachment), Maj. Henry W. Torbett; Veteran Reserve Corps, Col. Frank P. Cahill; 44th

Wisconsin (battalion), Lieut. Col. Oliver C. Bissell; 45th Wisconsin (battalion).

Garrison Artillery, Major John J. Ely—Illinois Light, Bridges's Battery, Lieut. Lyman A. White; Indiana Light, 2nd Battery, Capt. James S. Whicher; Indiana Light, 4th Battery, Capt. Benjamin F. Johnson; Indiana Light, 12th Battery, Capt. James E. White; Indiana Light, 21st Battery, Capt. Abram P. Andrew; Indiana Light, 22nd Battery, Capt. Edward W. Nicholson; Indiana Light, 24th Battery, Lieut. Hiram Allen; 1st Michigan Light, Battery F, Capt. Byron D. Paddock; 1st Ohio Light, Battery A, Lieut. Charles W. Scovill; 1st Ohio Light, Battery E, Lieut. Frank B. Reckard; Ohio Light, 20th Battery, Capt. William Backus; 1st Tennessee Light, Battery C, Lieut. Joseph Grigsby; 1st Tennessee Light, Battery D, Capt. Samuel D. Leinart; 2nd U. S. Colored Light, Battery A, Capt. Josiah V. Neigs.

Quartermaster's Division (composed of Quartermaster's employees), Bvt. Brig. Gen. James L. Donaldson

CAVALRY CORPS, Bvt. Maj. Gen. James H. Wilson

Escort—4th United States, Lieut. Joseph Hedges.

First Division [The Second and Third brigades of this division, under the division commander, Brig. Gen. E. M. McCook, were absent on an expedition into western Kentucky.]

First Brigade, Brig. Gen. John T. Croxton—8th Iowa, Col. James B. Dorr; 4th Kentucky (mounted infantry), Col. Robert M. Kelly; 2nd Michigan, Lieut. Col. Benjamin Smith; 1st Tennessee, Lieut. Col. Calvin M. Dyer; Illinois Light Artillery, Board of Trade Battery, Capt. George I. Robinson.

Fifth Division, Brig. Gen. Edward Hatch

First Brigade, Col. Robert R. Stewart—3rd Illinois,

Lieut. Col. Robert H. Carnahan; 11th Indiana, Lieut. Col. Abram Sharra; 12th Missouri, Col. Oliver Wells; 10th Tennessee, Maj. William P. Story.

Second Brigade, Col. Datus E. Coon—6th Illinois, Col. John Lynch; 7th Illinois, Maj. John M. Graham; 9th Illinois, Capt. Joseph W. Harper; 2nd Iowa, Maj. Charles C. Horton; 12th Tennessee, Col. George Spalding; 1st Illinois Light Artillery, Battery I, Lieut. Joseph A. McCartney.

Sixth Division, Brig. Gen. Richard W. Johnson

First Brigade, Col. Thomas J. Harrison—16th Illinois, Maj. Charles H. Beeres; 5th Iowa, Lieut. Col. Harlon Baird; 7th Ohio, Col. Israel Garrard.

Second Brigade, Col. James Biddle—14th Illinois, Maj. Haviland Tompkins; 6th Indiana, Maj. Jacob S. Stephens; 8th Michigan, Col. Elisha Mix; 3rd Tennessee, Maj. Benjamin Cunningham.

Artillery—4th United States, Battery I, Lieut. Frank G. Smith.

Seventh Division, Brig. Gen. Joseph F. Knipe

First Brigade, Bvt. Brig. Gen. John H. Hammond— 9th Indiana, Col. George W. Jackson; 10th Indiana, Lieut. Col. Benjamin Q. A. Gresham; 19th Pennsylvania, Lieut. Col. Joseph C. Hess; 2nd Tennessee, Lieut. Col. William R. Cook; 4th Tennessee, Lieut. Col. Jacob M. Thornburgh.

Second Brigade, Col. Gilbert M. L. Johnson—12th Indiana, Col. Edward Anderson; 13th Indiana, Lieut. Col. William T. Pepper; 6th Tennessee, Col. Fielding Hurst.

Artillery—Ohio Light, 14th Battery, Lieut. William C. Myers.

Organization of the Army of Tennessee

Commanded by General John B. Hood

December 10, 1864

INFANTRY

LEE'S CORPS, Lieut. Gen. Stephen D. Lee

Johnson's Division, Maj. Gen. Edward Johnson

Deas's Brigade, Brig. Gen. Zachariah C. Deas—19th Alabama, Lieut. Col. George R. Kimbrough; 22nd Alabama, Capt. H. W. Henry; 25th Alabama, Capt. Napoleon B. Rouse; 39th Alabama, Lieut. Col. William C. Clifton; 50th Alabama, Col. John G. Coltart.

Sharp's Brigade, Brig. Gen. Jacob H. Sharp—7th and 9th Mississippi, Maj. Henry Pope; 10th and 44th Mississippi and 9th Battalion Mississippi Sharpshooters, Capt. Robert A. Bell; 41st Mississippi, Capt. James M. Hicks.

Manigault's Brigade, Lieut. Col. William L. Butler—24th Alabama, Capt. Thomas J. Kimbell; 28th Alabama, Capt. William M. Nabors; 34th Alabama, Lieut. Col. John C. Carter; 10th South Carolina, Lieut. Col. C. Irvine Walker; 19th South Carolina, Capt. Thomas W. Getzen.

Brantley's Brigade, Brig. Gen. William F. Brantley—24th and 34th Mississippi, Capt. Clifton Dancy; 27th Mississippi, Capt. Samuel M. Pegg; 29th and 30th Mississippi, Capt. R. W. Williamson; Dismounted Calvary, Capt. D. W. Alexander.

Stevenson's Division, Maj. Gen. Carter L. Stevenson

Cumming's Brigade, Col. Elihu P. Watkins—34th Georgia, Capt. Russell A. Jones; 36th Georgia, Col. Charles E. Broyles; 39th Georgia, Capt. William P. Milton; 56th Georgia, Capt. Benjamin T. Spearman.

Pettus's Brigade, Brig. Gen. Edmund W. Pettus—20th Alabama, Col. James M. Dedman; 23rd Alabama, Lieut. Col. Joseph B. Bibb; 30th Alabama, Lieut. Col. James K. Elliott; 31st Alabama, Lieut. Col. Thomas M. Arrington; 46th Alabama, Capt. George E. Brewer.

Clayton's Division, Maj. Gen. Henry D. Clayton

Stovall's Brigade, Brig. Gen. Marcellus A. Stovall—40th Georgia, Col. Abda Johnson; 41st Georgia, Capt. Jared E. Stallings; 42nd Georgia, Col. Robert J. Henderson; 43rd Georgia, Col. Henry C. Kellogg; 52nd Georgia, Capt. Rufus R. Asbury.

Holtzclaw's Brigade, Brig. Gen. James T. Holtzclaw—18th Alabama, Lieut. Col. Peter F. Hunley; 32nd and 58th Alabama, Col. Bushrod Jones; 36th Alabama, Capt. Nathan M. Carpenter; 38th Alabama, Capt. Charles E. Bussey.

Gibson's Brigade, Brig. Gen. Randall L. Gibson—1st Louisiana, Capt. J. C. Stafford; 4th Louisiana, Col. Samuel E. Hunter; 13th Louisiana, Lieut. Col. Francis L. Campbell; 16th Louisiana, Lieut. Col. Robert H. Lindsay; 19th Louisiana, Maj. Camp Flournoy; 20th Louisiana, Capt. Alexander Dresel; 25th Louisiana, Col. Francis C. Zacharie; 30th Louisiana, Maj. Arthur Picolet; 4th Louisiana Battalion, Capt. T. A. Bisland; 14th Louisiana Battalion Sharpshooters, Lieut. A. T. Martin.

STEWART'S CORPS, Lieut. Gen. Alexander P. Stewart

Loring's Division, Maj. Gen. William W. Loring

Featherston's Brigade, Brig. Gen. Winfield S. Featherston—1st Mississippi, Capt. Owen D. Hughes; 3rd Mississippi, Capt. O. H. Johnston; 22nd Mississippi, Maj. Martin A. Oatis; 31st Mississippi, Capt. Robert A. Collins; 33rd Mississippi, Capt. T. L. Cooper; 40th Mississippi, Col. Wallace B. Colbert; 1st Mississippi Battalion, Maj. James M. Stigler.

Adams's Brigade, Col. Robert Lowry—6th Mississippi, Lieut. Col. Thomas J. Borden; 14th Mississippi, Col. Washington L. Doss; 15th Mississippi, Lieut. Col. James R. Binford; 20th Mississippi, Maj. Thomas B. Graham; 23rd Mississippi, Maj. George W. B. Garrett; 43rd Mississippi, Col. Richard Harrison.

Scott's Brigade, Col. John Snodgrass—55th Alabama, Maj. James B. Dickey; 57th Alabama, Maj. J. Horatio Wiley; 27th, 35th, and 49th Alabama (Consolidated), Lieut. Col. John D. Weeden; 12th Louisiana, Capt. James T. Davis.

French's Division, Maj. Gen. Samuel G. French

Ector's Brigade, Col. David Coleman—29th North Carolina, Maj. Ezekiel H. Hampton; 39th North Carolina, Capt. James G. Crawford; 9th Texas, Maj. James H. McReynolds; 10th Texas Cavalry (dismounted), Col. C. R. Earp; 14th Texas Cavalry (dismounted), Capt. Robert H. Harkey; 32nd Texas Cavalry (dismounted), Maj. William E. Estes.

Sears's Brigade, Brig. Gen. Claudius W. Sears—4th Mississippi; 35th Mississippi; 36th Mississippi; 39th Mississippi; 46th Mississippi; 7th Mississippi Battalion.

Cockrell's Brigade reported on detached service.

Walthall's Division, Maj. Gen. Edward C. Walthall

Quarles's Brigade, Brig. Gen. George D. Johnston—1st Alabama, Lieut. Charles M. McRae; 42nd, 46th,

49th, 53rd, and 55th Tennessee, Capt. Austin M. Duncan; 48th Tennessee, Col. William M. Voorhies.

Cantey's Brigade, Brig. Gen. Charles M. Shelley—17th Alabama, Capt. John Bolling, Jr.; 26th Alabama, Capt. D. M. Gideon; 29th Alabama, Capt. Samuel Abernethy; 37th Mississippi, Maj. Samuel H. Terrall.

Reynolds's Brigade, Brig. Gen. Daniel H. Reynolds—1st Arkansas Mounted Rifles (dismounted), Capt. R. P. Parks; 2nd Arkansas Mounted Rifles (dismounted), Maj. James P. Eagle; 4th Arkansas, Maj. Jesse A. Ross; 9th Arkansas, Capt. W. L. Phifer; 25th Arkansas, Lieut. T. J. Edwards.

CHEATHAM'S CORPS, Maj. Gen. Benjamin F. Cheatham

Brown's Division, [Commander not shown on return of December 10th]

Gist's Brigade, Col. Zachariah L. Watters—46th Georgia, Capt. Malcolm Gillis; 65th Georgia and 8th Georgia Battalion, Capt. William W. Grant; 2nd Georgia Battalion Sharpshooters, Capt. William H. Brown; 16th South Carolina, Capt. John W. Bolling; 24th South Carolina, Capt. W. C. Griffith.

Strahl's Brigade, Col. Andrew J. Kellar—4th, 5th, 31st, 33rd, and 38th Tennessee, Lieut. Col. Luke W. Finlay; 19th, 24th, and 41st Tennessee, Capt. Daniel A. Kennedy.

Maney's Brigade, Col. Hume R. Feild—4th (P.A.), 6th, 9th and 50th Tennessee, Lieut. Col. George W. Pease; 1st and 27th Tennessee, Lieut. Col. John L. House; 8th, 16th, and 28th Tennessee, Col. John H. Anderson.

Vaughan's Brigade, Col. William M. Watkins—11th and 29th Tennessee, Maj. John E. Binns; 12th and 47th

Tennessee, Capt. C. N. Wade; 13th, 51st, 52nd, and 154th Tennessee, Maj. John T. Williamson.

Cleburne's Division, Brig. Gen. James A. Smith

Govan's Brigade, Brig. Gen. Daniel C. Govan—1st, 2nd, 5th, 13th, 15th, and 24th Arkansas, Col. Peter V. Green; 6th and 7th Arkansas, Lieut. Col. Peter Snyder; 8th and 19th Arkansas, Maj. David H. Hamiter.

Lowrey's Brigade, Brig. Gen. Mark P. Lowrey—16th, 33rd, and 45th Alabama, Lieut. Col. Robert H. Abercrombie; 5th Mississippi and 3rd Mississippi Battalion, Capt. F. M. Woodward; 8th and 32nd Mississippi, Maj. Andrew E. Moody.

Granbury's Brigade, Capt. E. T. Broughton—5th Confederate, Lieut. William E. Smith; 35th Tennessee, Col. Benjamin J. Hill (?); 6th and 15th Texas, Capt. Benjamin R. Tyus; 7th Texas, Capt. O. P. Forrest; 10th Texas, Capt. R. D. Kennedy; 17th and 18th Texas Cavalry (dismounted), Capt. F. L. McKnight; 24th and 25th Texas Cavalry (dismounted), Capt. John F. Matthews; Nutt's (Louisiana) Cavalry Company, Capt. L. M. Nutt.

Smith's Brigade reported as on detached service.

Bate's Division, Brig. Gen. William B. Bate

Tyler's Brigade, Brig. Gen. Thomas Benton Smith—37th Georgia, Capt. James A. Sanders; 4th Georgia Battalion Sharpshooters, Maj. Theodore D. Caswell; 2nd, 10th, 20th, and 37th Tennessee, Lieut. Col. William M. Shy.

Finley's Brigade, Maj. Jacob A. Lash—1st and 3rd Florida, Capt. Matthew H. Strain; 6th Florida, Capt. Angus McMillan; 7th Florida, Capt. Robert B. Smith; 1st Florida Cavalry (dismounted) and 4th Florida Infantry, Capt. George R. Langford.

Jackson's Brigade, Brig. Gen. Henry R. Jackson—1st Georgia Confederate and 66th Georgia, Lieut. Col. James C. Gordon; 25th Georgia, Capt. Joseph E. Fulton; 29th and 30th Georgia, Col. William D. Mitchell; 1st Georgia Battalion Sharpshooters, Lieut. R. C. King.

ARTILLERY

LEE'S CORPS, Maj. John W. Johnston
Courtney's Battalion, Capt. James P. Douglas— Dent's (Alabama) battery, Capt. Staunton H. Dent; Douglas's (Texas) battery, Lieut. Ben Hardin; Garrity's (Alabama) battery, Lieut. Henry F. Carrell.
Eldridge's Battalion, Capt. Charles E. Fenner—Eufaula (Alabama) battery, Capt. William J. McKenzie; Fenner's (Louisiana) battery, Lieut. W. T. Clauveris; Stanford's (Mississippi) battery, Lieut. James S. McCall.
Johnston's Battalion, Capt. John B. Rowan—Corput's (Georgia) battery, Lieut. William S. Hoge; Marshall's (Tennessee) battery, Capt. Lucius G. Marshall; Stephens' (Georgia) Light Artillery, Lieut. William L. Ritter.

STEWART'S CORPS, Lieut. Col. Samuel C. Williams

Truehart's Battalion—Lumsden's (Alabama) battery; Selden's (Alabama) battery; Tarrant's (Alabama) battery.
Myrick's Battalion—Bouanchaud's (Louisiana) battery; Cowan's (Mississippi) battery; Darden's (Mississippi) battery.
Storrs's Battalion—Guibor's (Missouri) battery; Hoskins's (Mississippi) battery; Kolb's (Alabama) battery.

CHEATHAM'S CORPS, Col. Melancthon Smith

Hoxton's Battalion—Perry's (Florida) battery; Phelan's (Alabama) battery; Turner's (Mississippi) battery.
Hotchkiss's Battalion—Bledsoe's (Missouri) battery;

Goldthwaite's (Alabama) battery; Key's (Arkansas) battery.

Cobb's Battalion—Ferguson's (South Carolina) battery; Phillips's [Mebane's] (Tennessee) battery; Slocomb's (Louisiana) battery.

CAVALRY

CAVALRY DIVISION, Brig. Gen. James R. Chalmers

Escort Company, Capt. C. T. Smith.

Rucker's Brigade, Col. E. W. Rucker—7th Alabama; 5th Mississippi; 7th Tennessee; 14th Tennessee; 15th Tennessee; 26th Tennessee Battalion.

Biffle's Brigade, Col. Jacob B. Biffle—9th Tennessee; 10th Tennessee.

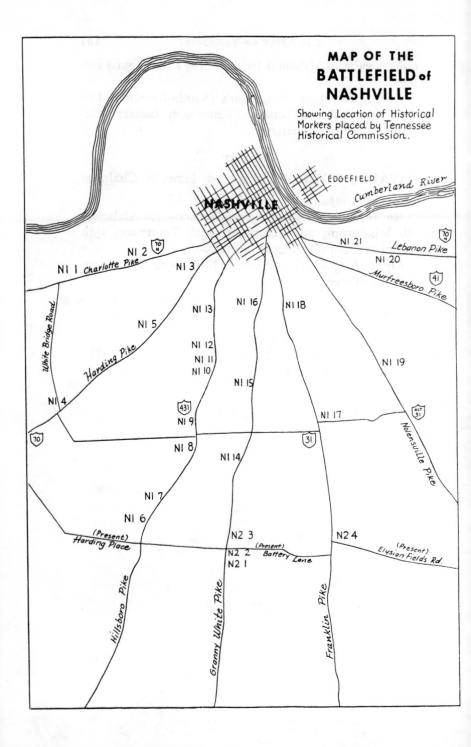

MAP OF THE
**BATTLEFIELD of
NASHVILLE**

Showing Location of Historical
Markers placed by Tennessee
Historical Commission.

Battle of Nashville

(December 15 & 16, 1864)

NOTE: All markers in this series are titled as above, with appropriate subtitles. Subtitles only are given below. Markers are listed as they occur on streets and highways leading out of Nashville, from west to east.

(Charlotte Ave., between 33rd & 35th Aves., near Immanuel Church of the Nazarene)

N1 2 CAVALRY ACTION—DECEMBER 15, 1864
The right of the main Federal defense line crossed Charlotte Pike here. In the opening phase of the battle, mounted and dismounted cavalry of Wilson's Corps moved out of the Federal works, supporting the advance of Smith's XVI Corps in a turning movement against the extreme left flank of the Confederate positions.

(Charlotte Pike, west of Richland Creek)

N1 1 CAVALRY ACTION—DECEMBER 15, 1864
Forming the outer arc of the Federal main attack, R. W. Johnson's 6th Cavalry Division, Wilson's Corps, here hit Rucker's Confederate Cavalry Brigade, west of Richland Creek. Withdrawing southward to Harding Road, Rucker held his ground there until bypassing Federal infantry forced further withdrawal to Hillsboro Pike late in the afternoon.

(In Centennial Park, in a grass plot near
parking space at Parthenon)
Nl 3   FEDERAL DEFENSES
The hill to the west was a strong point in the system of
permanent Federal defenses, started in 1862, which extended to the river on both sides of the town. Artillery
was emplaced here from time to time.

(West End Ave., at its intersection with Orleans Dr.)
Nl 5   XVI CORPS LINE OF DEPARTURE—
         DECEMBER 15, 1864
Supported by a division of Wilson's cavalry, A. J. Smith's
Corps moved westward astride Harding Road, displac-
ing Ector's Confederate Brigade from positions across
the pike northward to the west of Richland Creek. This
brigade outposted the Confederate left flank; the main
line was along the Hillsboro Pike.

(Harding Rd. [US 70] at junction with White Bridge Rd.)
Nl 4   DEFENSE BY ECTOR'S BRIGADE—
         DECEMBER 15, 1864
In position from here northward along high ground,
Ector's Brigade of French's Confederate Division, com-
manded by Col. Daniel Coleman, outposted the left of
Hood's line. Attacked by the Federal XVI Corps, sup-
ported by artillery and part of the Cavalry Corps, it was
overwhelmed. It withdrew southeast to Hillsboro Pike.

(21st Ave. S., at entrance to Vanderbilt Campus,
just north of Vanderbilt Hospital)
Nl 13   FEDERAL DEFENSES—
         DECEMBER 2–15, 1864
Near here, the interior defensive lines ran southwest to
cross Harding Pike; the total length of these works was

about 7 miles. First garrisoned by Wood's IV Corps, it was occupied December 15 by Donaldson's Division of Quartermaster employees. Part of the breastworks can be seen on Vanderbilt campus, 300 yards west.

(21st Ave. S., at intersection with Bernard Ave.)

N1   12   OUTER FEDERAL DEFENSES—
           DECEMBER 2, 1864

Here the outer Federal defensive line, which stretched 7 miles around the city, crossed Hillsboro Pike. It was used at the commencement of the battle on December 15 by Wood's IV Corps as a line of departure for the main attack. Faint traces of the old entrenchments are visible a few yards west.

(21st Ave. S., at intersection with Linden Ave.)

N1   11   IV CORPS JUMP-OFF LINE—
           DECEMBER 15, 1864

Using the defensive salient 500 yards east, Wood's Corps, with the XVI Corps on its right, swung southwest to envelop the left of the Confederate line, 1½ miles south, and pushed it back in spite of determined resistance. The XXIII Corps (Schofield) followed in support.

(21st Ave. S., at intersection with Cedar Lane)

N1   10   ASSAULT ON MONTGOMERY HILL—
           DECEMBER 15, 1864

500 yards east of here, Maj. Gen. T. J. Wood led an assault by his IV Corps against the Confederate skirmish line on the hill, eventually carrying it. Attacking the main line about 600 yards south, Wood was unable to take it by direct assault, the divisions of Loring and Walthall holding fast until the XVI Corps, moving past their left, forced withdrawal.

(State Route 106, near intersection with Hampton Ave.)

N1 9 REDOUBT NO. 1—DECEMBER 15, 1864
Stewart's Confederate Corps held this salient of the left of Hood's defenses. A thin infantry line ran south behind a stone wall on the east side of the pike. After the routing of Ector's Brigade on Harding Pike, and successive overrunning of Redoubts 3, 4, and 5 to the south, Stewart's position was flanked; he withdrew southeast toward Granny White Pike.

(State Route 106, about 100 yards south of intersection with Woodmont Blvd.)

N1 8 CONFEDERATE OUTPOST—
DECEMBER 15, 1864
100 yards west was Redoubt No. 3 in the Confederate system of detached works beyond the main line. It was overrun by the enveloping attack of Wood's IV Corps from the northwest.

(State Route 106, at intersection with Hobbs Rd.)

N1 7 LUMSDEN'S DEFENSE—
DECEMBER 15, 1864
0.3 mile west was Redoubt No. 4 in Hood's detached supporting works. Garrisoned by Lumsden's Battery of smoothbore Napoleons, supported by 100 men of the 29th Alabama Infantry under Capt. Foster, it was finally overrun by the assault of 12 infantry and 4 dismounted cavalry regiments, supported by 4 Federal batteries.

(State Route 106, about 0.8 mile south of N 17)

N1 6 TAKING OF REDOUBT NO. 5—
DECEMBER 15, 1864
Hood's Redoubt No. 5 was on this hill. Couch's division of the XXIII Corps, sweeping to the south of the route of Smith's XVI, captured it and the hills to the east late in the afternoon. Wilson's cavalry, crossing the highway

about 2 miles south, advanced rapidly eastward, flanking the Confederate defenses.

(12th Ave. S., south of intersection with
Acklen Ave., about opposite #2016)

**N1   16   SCHOFIELD'S JUMP-OFF LINE—
DECEMBER 15, 1864**

The Federal defensive line ran northeast and southwest through here. It was garrisoned by Schofield's Corps on arrival here after the Battle of Franklin, December 2, and later became a line of departure for the advance into support positions: Cruft's Provisional Division then occupied this line in reserve.

(12th Ave. S., about 75 yards south of its
intersection with Woodmont Blvd.)

**N1   15   CONFEDERATE DEFENSES—
DECEMBER 15, 1864**

Stewart's Corps, Army of Tennessee, held this part of Hood's original line, extending east about 1500 yards, and west and south about 1 mile to Hillsboro Pike. After the turning of his left, about 4:00 p.m., Stewart established a new position extending southward, to the west of Granny White Pike.

(Granny White Pike, near intersection
with Shackleford Rd.)

**N1   14   CONFEDERATE DEFENSES—
DECEMBER 15, 1864**

After being outflanked by the advance of the Federal XVI Corps (Smith), Loring and Walthall put their divisions in a defensive line west of this road, facing westward. Here, their determined defense brought Federal advances against the Confederate left to a close for the day.

*(Granny White Pike, opposite southeast corner
of Burton School grounds)*

N2   3   SCHOFIELD'S ASSAULT—
DECEMBER 16, 1864

The Federal XXIII Corps attacked southeastward from
positions about ¾ mile west. Coordinating with the attack of Smith's XVI Corps, and assisted by pressure by
Wilson's encircling cavalry from the south, its action
brought about the final collapse of Hood's defenses.

*(Granny White Pike, about 150 yards
south of Burton School)*

N2   2   SMITH'S ASSAULT—DECEMBER 16, 1864

The Federal XVI Corps attacked southward along this
road. After violent artillery bombardment, McArthur's
Division took the hill to the west about 4:00 p.m., pre-
cipitating the rout of Hood's Army. This hill is named
for Col. W. M. Shy, 20th Tenn. Inf., killed in the desperate defense which he commanded.

(Granny White Pike, at intersection with Sewanee Rd.)

N2   1   CONFEDERATE POSITION—
DECEMBER 16, 1864

Stewart's Corps, badly mauled during the first day, withdrew at night to a line extending eastward. Lee's Corps,
forming the right wing, extended the line across the
Franklin Pike. Cheatham's Corps, on Stewart's left,
extended the line westward, and following the hills,
curved south. Chalmers' Cavalry Division covered the
left flank.

*(8th Ave. S., on south slope of hill on
which sits the City Reservoir)*

N1   18   FEDERAL DEFENSIVE LINE—
DECEMBER 15, 1864

The Federal defensive line ran NE and SW through here.

Fort Casino was on the hill to the west, Fort Negley to the northeast. Garrisoned on December 2 by Schofield's XXIII Corps, it was occupied by Cruft's Provisional Division when the battle began. The XXIII Corps moved out in support of the main effort, 5 miles southwest.

*(State Route 6, near battle monument
at intersection with Thompson Lane)*

N1 17   LEE'S POSITION—DECEMBER 15, 1864
Here, Stephen D. Lee's Corps, Army of Tennessee, bestrode the highway and railroad. Cheatham's Corps held the right of the line, which ran northeast about 2 miles to Rains' Hill. After the Confederate left was broken in the afternoon's fighting, Lee's Corps fell back to high ground about 1½ miles south.

*(State Route 6, north of intersection
with Elysian Fields Rd.)*

N2 4   CONFEDERATE DEFENSES—
DECEMBER 16, 1864
Lee's Corps held the right flank of the line in the final stages of the battle, linking with Stewart to the west. Here it extended east, then south around Peach Orchard Hill. Violent attacks by Steedman's brigades were repulsed bloodily; Lee did not withdraw until the left and center of the Confederate line had collapsed.

(4th Ave. S., at Peachtree St.)

N1 19   CHEATHAM'S LINE—
DECEMBER 15, 1864
Holding a line running northeast and southwest and with its right on the N.C. and St. L.R.R. at Rains' Cut, Cheatham's Confederate Corps stood off the attacks of Steedman's brigades. Part of Cheatham's Corps was moved to the support of Stewart's left late in the after-

noon: collapse of the left wing forced Cheatham's withdrawal southward during the night.

(Hermitage Ave., near entrance to City Hospital)

N1   21   STEEDMAN'S LINE OF DEPARTURE—
DECEMBER 15, 1864

The left of the Federal main defensive line rested on the Cumberland River north of here, extending southeast to the Murfreesboro Pike. From this line, Steedman's Provisional Detachment of six brigades made the secondary attack against the Confederate right. Thomas' main attack was delivered against the Confederate left.

(Lafayette St., at intersection with Claiborne St.)

N1   20   STEEDMAN'S POSITION—
DECEMBER 15, 1864

From a line of departure running northeast-southwest through here, Maj. Gen. Steedman's Provisional Detachment of 6 brigades at 6:00 a.m. launched a holding attack southwestward against the Confederate right, on high ground about 2 miles south. The main attack, about 5 miles west, enveloped the Confederate left after an all-day fight.